A PILOT'S PASSION

Baseball Travels the World

Written by
SCOTT R. WEAVER

Edited by
KRISTIN "KJ" JOHNSON

LB Aero Publication, LLC

Washington D.C.

ISBN: 978 – 0 – 578 – 74216 – 8

Printed in the United State of America

Table of Contents

Dedication

To my family for their continuing support and especially my dad, RC "Doc" Weaver, for introducing me to the great game of baseball. I want to reach out and thank my wingman and editor, Kristin "KJ" Johnson whose insight, feedback, and passion for writing helped keep this project rounding the bases. Although my name is on the front of the book, the real thanks go to the contributors and ballplayers, who knocked it out of the park.

Thank you.

Matt Blackmore, David Burns, Liam Carroll, Chris Maloney, Lisa Maulden, Eric Niesen, Paul Perry, Alex Pike, Omar Prieto, Pablo Tesouro, Jonathan Weaver

The Weaver family at a Washington Nationals Playoff game.

Epigram

"Love is the most important thing in the world, but baseball is pretty good, too"
Yogi Berra, New York Yankees

*Jon, Syb, Lianne and Scott. Father-Son
Baseball Classic 2016*

Foreword

By Scott & Jonathan Weaver

Jon and Scott. Shirley Povich Field. 2017

Scott

Like most of the contributors to this book, I was first introduced to the game of baseball by playing catch with my dad. He was a pilot for the USAF and at the time he was working with NASA to help put a man in the moon. I later went on to play and coach at several levels, to include Little League, High School, American League, College, Semi-pro, and even was invited to a tryout by the Los Angeles Dodgers and Cincinnati Reds.

But I didn't realize just how important the game was to me until I nearly lost the son I knew.

In 2005, my son Jonathan, often called "JoJo," "Joe" or "Jon," was nineteen years old and a freshman at the University of Maryland. One night, he called.

He said, "Dad, I'm having trouble sleeping."

The campus was only forty minutes away, so I did what any father would do. I drove over there. When I first laid eyes on him, he looked disheveled, eyes dilated, pitch black, like he was on drugs. But he was laser focused, coherent and but nervous. I knew something was wrong.

I asked him, point-blank, "What are you taking?"

"Maybe…a little weed."

Right.

I was concerned, but maybe it was time for the "swift kick in the ass." talk. But somehow, I knew this was not the time to pull out that lecture.

I leaned against the car while Jonathan nervously paced. He was carrying a full load of courses and playing club baseball. Maybe he had too much on his plate.

We made small talk about classes, girls, baseball workouts, staying active, healthy diet, but mainly about limiting the "party" scene. But I could tell he wasn't really listening. I was lost.

I reluctantly got in my car and headed home only to have the phone ring three hours later. Jo was nearly in tears when I answered the phone. He said, "Dad, I'm sorry I didn't tell you this before, but I haven't slept in three days! I'm scared. Can you come get me?"

I knew we needed to get Jonathan evaluated, but for what? Drugs? Gretchen, my wife, was working at National Institute of Health (NIH). The morning after I brought Jo home, Gretchen picked up the phone and made a few calls. By afternoon we had been referred and I was explaining the story to one of the top mental health experts in the Washington D.C. region.

I described Jo's behavior, a strange combination of depression and anxiety. She asked basic health related questions. What medications or drugs was he on? Overall health? Family history?

Fifteen minutes later, she was quick and to the point. "I believe your son has bipolar disorder. I'd like to meet him in person as soon as possible."

The words dropped on me like a MK-84 or a 2000-pound bomb.

Bipolar?

I'd heard the term bipolar before, but I never truly understood what it meant. Ups and downs. Cycles. Medication. Counseling. It was all a blur. It would take me years to get my arms around the severity of this devastating illness. You don't just take a pill, get some counseling and come out on the other side cured.

Quickly, we got Jonathan on a medication protocol and set up counseling. We kept our fingers crossed that everything was going to be normal after this one incident. It took several months, but Jonathan eventually came back down from his manic episode and now we were warned to watch out for the swing of the depressive or the darker side of the bipolar illness. The medication shut down the manic episode and drove it into darkness and depression: hoodie 24/7, sleeping long hours, shaded bedrooms, difficulty getting to class.

Six months later, Jonathan seemed to be doing better. He had cycled through his low and depressive episode, was attending class, working out with the baseball team and seemed to be back on course. But then....

It was a hot summer Friday night in Maryland when I got a call from one of Jo's friends, whose voice was full of panic. "Mr. Weaver, Jonathan is out of control, acting weird and scaring people. Can we bring him home?"

The doorbell rang. Gretchen and I opened up the door.

Jonathan was being held firmly by two friends. Eyes wide open and dilated again. Black. But instead of long blond hair, as we last saw him, his head was completely shaven. And not only his head, his entire body and even his eyebrows too.

There was sheer panic and fear in his friends' eyes. They said, "Mr. Weaver, we don't know what's going on, but he's not right."

Episode two had just occurred. There would be more to come.

When Jonathan was manic, he had difficulty standing or sitting still. He would pace. Sometimes when he couldn't sleep, he'd get up in the middle of the night, start brewing coffee, bang around the kitchen as if everyone in the house was wide awake like his over active mind was or he'd just wander off on his own or even drive himself to go buy a pack of smokes. When Jo was manic, no one slept.

Other than time, medication and a cigarette, there was something else that seemed to help him settle his nerves and stay focused for a just few minutes: playing catch.

Who would have thought the answer would lie in the simple game fathers have taught their sons over the decades? Ball to glove and repeat. I always had a couple of gloves and baseballs around, and the simple game of playing catch with a baseball helped to quiet his mind. Slow it down. Help focus. Dozens of times we played catch, manic episode or not. The bonding. The connection. Father to son, son to father. Back and forth. The rhythm of playing catch seemed to help, even if it was just for a few minutes. But we'd take whatever we could get.

It was around the first or second episode that the concept of a Father-Son Baseball Classic as a part of our family's annual tradition was born. Most of the guys I played with at the time had been coaches when their kids were younger. Most of the kids were in college now. I needed a positive connection with Jo and thought it would be a great opportunity for all of us grown guys, many who still played in "old man" leagues, to have with our sons.

Within a few weeks, I had selected a date, located a field, found sponsors, hired umpires and started contacting players. We had eight teams, raised money, and started the first annual Father-Son Baseball Classic in the Washington D.C. area.

FSB logo. Founded in 2006

It's now 2021 and last year we were going to celebrate our fifteenth annual Father-Son Baseball Classic in, of all places, London, England, but due to the COVID-19 virus we had to cancel our trip (see the related story later in this book).

On the upside, I'm happy to say that Jonathan is living a healthy lifestyle and doing well. He lives and works in the Raleigh, North Carolina area, has a beautiful girlfriend Claire, and plays golf and, yes still plays baseball.

Jo

I remember my first full-blown episode, mostly from stories from the people closest to me. The simplest way for me to describe it is a Fourth of July fireworks show with your neurons that goes on for weeks, sometimes months. Fantastic and awe-inspiring at first, but a marathon of a sprint.

I remember during one episode I was throwing long toss by myself into a fence on tennis court in my father's residential neighborhood at four in morning when he came for me. Wide-eyed, he asked me, "What the heck are ya doing, kid?"

I said, "I'm trying to get tired. I can't sleep."

He somehow reeled off, and we turned that into playing catch. It worked. When I would try to fire a fastball through his glove at 45 feet he would, palms down, push both hands down to calm me the way a catcher would work a pitcher when he's overthrowing. Where words were hard to find, baseball's international language translated.

My episodes were usually triggered in the summer months. Longer days, more activity and less sleep would spin me out of control. As my dad explained, we came together and organized a weekend in August which turned into a sort of a yearly check-in, with the focus around a game we loved. Father-Son Baseball became a sort of metronome and a goal to look forward to. I used it as motivation to be in good enough mental shape enough to play. A decade of games.

The yearly snapshot pictures became timestamps like those pictures they sell at amusement parks when on the roller coaster when you hit the biggest drop. I wasn't always manic, but sometimes I was. We would look back at pictures and I would have conversations with my dad.

"Here you were very manic," he would say.

I would respond, "Was I really?" Episodes become blurs and flashes from my perspective.

Dad would say something along the lines of, "You tried to hit left-handed and laid a drag bunt down when we were up eight runs." To translate from baseball language: I was acting like a fool!

As you can see, Father-Son Baseball didn't cure my illness. Nothing will. But longevity and keeping in mind that I had a goal to play in a game became milestones I sought after. Not to impress my dad, but to learn to stay grounded with a familiar sport and its fundamentals.

My struggle helped me in several ways. What I brought most to teammates and coaches in my international play was not an unbelievable talent, it was mental fortitude spawned from always having a positive attitude. Where French players would drop their heads after mistakes, I would pick them up through lessons I had learned. I used these tools given to me from being humbled by this great game, and without a doubt my dad picked me up when I failed.

My dad had a shirt that read "Baseball Is Life," and I learned life is a lot like baseball. You are bound to fail and slump. Nobody cares about your statistics, but everyone notices how you bounce back and reach for the team's next win.

Coaches tee-shirt

I am grateful to my dad and grateful to my family. I'm also grateful to be healthy and still play baseball, the game I love.

Scott and Jo

Now enjoy the stories from ballplayers from around the world, learn about finding your passion and maybe a few lessons learned in A Pilot's Passion: Baseball Travels the World.

.

Introduction

By Scott "Hurler" Weaver

In 2017 I published my first book called <u>The Pilots of Thunderbird Field.</u> It was really just a book to capture some of the stories and memories of my grandfather, who was a flight instructor in World War II in a place called Thunderbird Field in and around Phoenix, Arizona. I mainly wrote the book just for family's sake.

But when the book was published, it received accolades from aviation historians and the book did surprisingly well in select Amazon categories. After the family ended up buying the first dozen or so copies, we ended up selling several thousand hard, paperback and eBook versions without much marketing. But writing the book opened up some other unexpected opportunities.

At the time, a good friend of mine, Barry Sandler, who's been in sales all his life in and around Washington D.C., read the book and loved it and invited me to speak to his sales staff up around Columbia, Maryland, just south of Baltimore, Maryland.

And I said, "Well, Barry, what the hell am I going to talk about to your group?"

And he said, "Just tell them stories about your flying career and the Air Force as an F-16 fighter pilot, and your stories about baseball and your travel around the world and some lessons learned." Barry always reminded me that he had the "right stuff" to be a fighter pilot! But instead he was in sales.

I had about two weeks to prepare. I'd done some public speaking in front of U.S. Air Force fighter squadrons during the Cold War, so it was simple to put together a couple of slides, tell some interesting stories, and make it relevant to today's business environment. One thing led to another and opened the door to some public speaking with the renowned Hall of Fame speaker Lt. Col. Rob "Waldo" Waldman at Wingman Enterprises over the next couple of years. I had several opportunities to speak to different kinds of clients around the U.S. to include bankers, financiers, contractors and many more companies. Thanks, Waldo, for your mentorship!

Lt. Col. Scott "Hurler" Weaver. Keynote speaker Atlanta, Georgia. 2018

I always started off my presentations with one comment. The gist of the comment was, "Besides family, I have two passions in my life: baseball and aviation." I've been involved with aviation and baseball for the past fifty years, playing and coaching and being on a ball field and continuing to play, coach, manage and sponsor well into adulthood.

Because of these passions—family, aviation, and baseball—this book has been developing in my mind for over ten years, but I never had the time or space to work on it. When the Covid-19 pandemic hit in early 2020, I was basically grounded. There was hardly any flying domestically and almost near zero flying internationally. My wife Gretchen, an attorney at the National Institute of Health outside of D.C., was working from home and my fourteen-year old daughter Lianne was completing her 8th grade class work online as well as participating in other activities such as modern dance, ballet, American Sign Language (ASL) and Mandarin. She paints and writes constantly, even working on her own series of short stories! What was my excuse for not writing my second book? There was none.

Lianne cheering on the Georgetown Hoyas baseball team.

18

The time I was on a leave of absence (LOA) gave me time to think about the goal(s) for this book, <u>A Pilot's Passion</u>: Baseball Travels the World. The purpose is to share our experiences, from outstanding "baseball" people and maybe a few lessons learned from flying, playing and coaching baseball over 50+ years. More importantly, this book gives me an outlet for sharing some of the very unique people I had an opportunity to meet in places like Argentina, Brazil, England, France, Japan and Spain. Many of them will tell you in their chapters that I gave them the opportunity to share a sport with people who, in many cases, are more passionate about the game than myself. Finally, as you've read, it's my aim to share how baseball has helped our family in our struggle with mental health, in hopes that we can bring better awareness and reduce the social stigma attached to such a brutal disease.

<u>A Pilot's Passion: Baseball Travels the World</u> focuses on a handful of colorful individuals, leaders and adventurers with whom I crossed paths during my travels around the world. As a 777-200 wide body, international pilot with American Airlines, one of the most frequent questions I get from "non-flyers" are how long are your layovers, do you have to pay for the hotels, how much time to you get off on your trip and what do you normally do with your time? Most layovers are around 24-hours and many crew members will say catch up on sleep, work out, see a sight or two, grab a beer and a meal before flying back home. My goal was to see if I could find out where the "locals" were playing baseball. From London to Buenos Aires, Tokyo to Paris, and a little help from the "Google machine," I was able to find a small niche of people playing baseball wherever I was.

The goal of this book is to introduce you to a few of these quirky individuals and what they taught me along the way. For example, you'll meet Paul Perry, the self-proclaimed "Godfather of Baseball in Buenos Aires," Liam Carroll, former head coach of the Great Britain National team and his efforts to qualify for the 2020 (now 2021) Olympics as well as his goal of developing baseball in the entire Great Britain region. And then there's Pablo Tesouro, who played his college ball in Missouri and now his passion and drive are to revitalize a professional league in Northern Argentina. I'm convinced each and every one of these individuals has a book in them and I am so thankful they shared part of their story with me. I've made friendships that will last a life time and truly appreciative of their contributions.

Amongst the chapters are some lessons learned from these passionate individuals, coaches, and mentors, as well as some lessons I learned as instructor pilot in the U.S. Air Force and as a commercial airline pilot. As a player, coach, manager and pilot, I started to see similarities in flying and baseball world and the importance of having a "wingman" or teammates. Some may think it's a stretch to say flying, an F-16C in a three-dimensional space and throwing a baseball from 60' 6" are comparable, but the mindset is the same. The approach to the game and lessons about preparation, management, leadership skills, goal-setting, and the emotional intelligence involved with the game of baseball or flying combat missions can be applied to many business situations and to our day-to-day lives.

Father-Son Baseball Classic 2018. Lots of smiling faces.

Lefty takes the mound during spring training

When writing about lessons learned, I enlisted an incredible coach, teacher and former professional pitcher for the New York Mets organization, Coach Eric "Lefty" Niesen. He is the former pitching coach at Georgetown University. Together we break down our takeaways from the game of baseball from Lefty's perspective as a professional pitcher and coach and my perspective as a fighter pilot, on how improve your mental approach to the game and maybe other aspects of your life.

You won't be disappointed in the adventures and stories of ballplayers within these covers. Again, I'm fortunate to have met and made lifelong friends along my flight path and travels discovering baseball around this globe. Enjoy the book!

Europe: Journeys from New York (JFK) to London-Heathrow (LHR), UK

Chapter 1

Baseball and the "Triple 7"- London (LHR) Bound by Scott "Hurler" Weaver (USA)

Callsigns in the military are commonplace. Some are simple, some are crude, some funny and some clever. But the more you liked your callsign, the less likely it would stay with you.

I went through several in my 20+ year career as an officer in the United States Air Force. I was a T-38A instructor pilot out of undergraduate pilot training (UPT), followed by the F-16C for most of my career.

"Weav" was my first callsign. Just a truncated version of my last name, like Fish or Abe. During my first assignment in the F-16C or "Viper" as the line pilots referred to the jet, I was called "Dream" after the cheesy 1975 song "Dream Weaver" written by Gary Wright. I learned then that the more you hated a callsign the longer it stuck with you. Dream stuck with me for three long years!

Later, I was called "Hurler". Now I know what you're thinking, he must have a weak stomach when it comes to flying around at 1.5 Mach and pulling Gs! But that was not the case. I picked up the call sign "Hurler" from a squadron mate in the D.C. Air National Guard based out of Andrews Joint Navy and AFB. Hurler didn't come from throwing up in the cockpit, but instead came from my love for baseball. I would often change from a flight suit into a baseball uniform in time to get to the next game!

When I left the active duty in the early 90s and moved from my last duty assignment at Hahn Air Base, Germany (formerly known as West Germany) to the Washington, D.C. area, I soon discovered there were men's baseball leagues playing actual hardball or baseball and rediscovering my love for baseball.

Colorado University Baseball, 1979

In the meantime, my firstborn son, Jonathan or Jon/Joe/JoJo, was starting to play T-ball, recreational and travel baseball in the Cal Ripken League or Little League equivalent in Maryland. So, when I wasn't flying with the 727-200, MD-80 or the F-16C, you could find me on the baseball field either playing or coaching. As a youth coach our program had some success winning the Maryland State Championship three years in a row and finishing runner-up the fourth year. Looking back, it was one of the greatest memories, friendships and learning experiences of my life. I had the opportunity to work with young people and teach them the basics of the game, specifically how to enjoy the game and just play the game to have fun. Winning was never the priority. Although no one made it to the "big leagues," many of the players moved on to enjoy successful high school and college careers.

As I mentioned, Hurler is another slang name for pitcher. So, in my 30s and 40s I got back into pitching. Before all of that, I was an All-State player from the small state of New Mexico as a middle infielder and pitcher. The Los Angeles Dodgers and the Cincinnati Reds invited me to closed tryouts but before the MLB draft, I signed a letter of intent to pitch at the University of Colorado.

As a pitcher at Colorado, I had some minor success. I was a two-year letterman, 50+ innings of mainly relief, but the occasional weekend starter, I had a 2-3 career win-loss record and a respectable 5.24 ERA in the new metal bat era and the high altitude of Colorado. But my mechanics were not fluid. I had a quick or rushed delivery. Hips and shoulders flew open a touch early, putting stress on the arm. I could often be found after an outing with two bags of ice. One on my shoulder and the other on my elbow with a Coors beer in my free hand. Coors was a "local" brewery in Colorado and only allowed to sell 3.2% beer. Time for a quick joke! What do making love in a canoe and drinking Coors 3.2% (lite) beer have in common? They're both fucking close to water! I promise, there will be no more jokes!

Having rediscovered pitching in my mid-30's, I needed to improve. In the late 1990s, pre-Internet, coaches were starting to produce excellent videos about pitching and other aspects of the game. Quality stuff if you had a VHS player to watch it back then!

Flash forward to my coaching days. As a coach I was teaching the basic skills of the game to young players. As a player, I was retooling my mechanics to play. The combination of coach and player was beneficial because it reminded me how difficult the game is to play, but more importantly to be thankful and happy every chance I got to step on the field.

As I continued to travel around the world as a pilot, I had an opportunity to stay involved with the game of baseball, both on the field and off the field. Whether it was delivering used baseball gear to a church group in Argentina or something less pious like "smuggling" in a can or two of Copenhagen Smokeless tobacco to London. The game was about friendships and the common passion for the game we all love.

On my layovers, I sought out the baseball fields and, more importantly, the baseball managers and players who've exported their love for the game in places most would not have thought the game was ever played. From Australia to Argentina. London to Paris.

My initial check out in the Boeing 777-200 in 1999, my first flight out to London from JFK, was with a Captain Greg Knapp. A great guy. Greg was what we called a "Kid Captain," meaning he was hired when he was 22 or 23 years old in the 1980s. He was a 727 captain when he was maybe 25 years old. He was a "fast burner," went on to become a Check Airman or instructor at the Flight Academy at American Airlines and ascended to the top of the management team by the time he was in his mid-30s. Now at the ripe old age of 50, he is in charge of all the training for the 777 and 787 for a major international airline. He has done everything in the company. He has been a check airman, a flight instructor, and he's been a managing flight officer.

Captain Knapp was my instructor for my IEO (initial check out) from New York's Kennedy Airport (JFK) to London Heathrow Airport (LHR). Our flight plan time from JFK to London-Heathrow was less than eight hours, so we were only planned as a two-man crew. Anything over eight hours is normally three crew members and over twelve hours flight time is four crew members. Today it was just Captain Knapp and myself. Having been a domestic guy for the past eighteen years, meaning only flying in the United States and occasionally the Caribbean islands, flying the Atlantic into complex British airspace around London was going to make for a long day.

AA 777-200. First trip to London.

Captain Knapp by nature is a talker, and he started the pre-brief three hours prior to departure time. The flight deck preflight another 90 minutes. We did a walkaround, and it was the first time I'd ever seen the outside of a 777. Greg did the walkaround showing me all the important items. Then we got to the cockpit and setting up the computer and the flight management system. It was a 7-hour and 55-minute flight time with all of the instruction being taught by Captain Knapp. It is always great learning new things, but it was a long day/night. It was draining, not stressful, just draining.

777-200 cockpit out of JFK.

The challenging thing about flying to London is, you take off around 9:00 p.m. body time, but watch the sun rise over Europe just a few hours later. Your body clock starts to wake up as the sun is pounding your windscreen. Landing is very complex, and you now have to understand a new accent, the British accents. London controllers are just that, very controlling. They're very precise, and you have to repeat back clearances exactly the way they say them. It's a stressful arrival coming into London.

Off to the 1.5-hour bus ride in rush hour traffic to the Holiday Inn Forum in downtown Kensington part of London. I was exhausted by the time I got there at 9:30 or 10:00 am. London time. Captain Knapp was notorious for taking the newbies on these trips to London to every pub, every restaurant and every music place in London. So right before we go to bed he said, "Hey, we'll all meet downstairs at the pub at 6:00 p.m., get some dinner and I'll show you a couple of places in the local area. Churchill's is a famous pub that's just a couple of blocks away."

I told him I was going to skip going out to dinner, and he looked at me and his eyes opened up and he said, "Well, why?"

I replied, "I'm off to play baseball with a team called the London Mets. I brought two dozen baseballs and some chewing tobacco. I'm going to take the Piccadilly Line and go up to Finsbury Park. I'm going to introduce myself to some of the players that play with the London Mets."

That was my first introduction to baseball in London. A couple of weeks before the flight to London, I did a Google search. The London Mets came up as well as contact information for the manager, named Alex Pike, an Aussie transplant. I was able to reach out to Alex Pike, and he said in an Aussie accent, "Yeah, mate, we'd love to have an American coming over and bring us some supplies." What a great welcome to baseball, in all places, London, England. You'll read Pikey's story later, but he was like many club team managers around the world. Manager, player and team social director. He was recently inducted into the London Mets Hall of Fame for his hitting skills!

As it turned out, I guess the baseballs were a hard commodity for the Brits to get because they don't have sporting goods stores that carry baseballs. Because of that, they'll play with baseballs till they turn muddy brown. The dip or chewing tobacco is for some reason not imported and can't be bought legally in England. I ended up becoming a baseball mule and establishing great relationships that have lasted a long time.

The following stories are from individuals that I've met on my travels through Europe.

David Burns, a Canadian, is the founder of Baseball Jobs Overseas. Living in Austria, Burns has helped me and other club teams around the world, how to locate, recruit and negotiate with baseball players to play in semi-professional and club baseball around the world.

Liam Carroll is another storyteller. I have watched Liam develop over the last ten years and become one of the shining stars of coaching and one of the best managers of baseball in Europe.

Then last not least, my son Jonathan Weaver's experience as an American playing for the French National Team and later played at the University of Maryland's club team.

But first, a father-son baseball story.

Father-Son Baseball: London Bound

In 2018, Major League Baseball announced that the New York Yankees and the Boston Red Sox would play two games in London in a soccer facility in the MLB London Series.

Scott and Liam at the NY Yankees vs Boston Red Sox. 60,000 international fans in London. 2019.

I was on the 777 flying back and forth to London. And it would be easy for me to hold a weekend trip. In the summer of 2019, I bought a ticket to go to a Saturday Yankees-Red Sox game in London on June 29. My good friend Liam Carroll, the head coach of the Great Britain National Team who you'll meet later in this section, was going to be involved with the (MLB) major leagues' sponsorship of the game over there, as well as the London Mets. The Yankees donated $25,000 worth of gear to their youth program up in Finsbury Park before this happened.

I flew in from Miami on Friday and got in that Saturday morning. Out of the crew that I was flying with, one guy was interested in going. He bought a ticket online and, after a quick nap at the hotel, we went and watched the New York Yankees in a slugfest, with the Yankees winning 17-13. The Yankees beat the Red Sox in both games. It was outstanding and the game was sold out with 60,000 people in attendance.

And it gave me an idea.

I knew that the following year, 2020, that the St. Louis Cardinals and the Chicago Cubs were going back to play in the same facility. And having known Liam and the London Mets organization, I said, "Why don't we have our fifteenth Father-Son Baseball tournament in London?"

You learned about the Father-Son Baseball Classic in detail in the foreword. This is a tradition that has lasted for fifteen years. I immediately got on my roster of ten to fifteen guys that I know and whose sons might be interested. I got a resounding, "Yes! Sign us up! We're on our way!"

We had scheduled the game to play against the London Mets on June 12, 2020. The London Mets had just won the European Club Championship and were going to be playing in 2020. They were preparing to enter a European Cup Tournament and were happy to have a friendly game with us.

We rented a place through Airbnb. During one of my trips to London, I met a local lawyer who was going to rent us a place that had six bedrooms, because it could sleep twelve people. We were going to pile a bunch of fathers and sons in for the fifteenth annual Father-Son Baseball Classic.

Unfortunately, the COVID-19 pandemic started in March and April 2020. Quickly, seasons got cancelled. The MLB eventually cancelled the start of their season for 2020 in early May and we ended up having to cancel our Father-Son Classic in Europe.

It will probably be the end of the Father-Son Baseball Classic because most of the dads now are in their sixties, including myself, and physically it's going to be difficult for us to stay together and play competitive baseball anymore. But our sons will have the chances when they start their families.

Chapter 2

Don't Try Too Hard to be "The Guy" by David Burns (Canada/Austria)

David Burns. Founder of Baseball Jobs Overseas.

Don't Try Too Hard to be "The Guy"

I am the founder of Baseball Jobs Overseas, a platform and service dedicated to helping aspiring or established baseball players and coaches take their career overseas. We also do the same for women's fastpitch, but softball is about 1/100th of the size of the business we do in baseball.

Like some of the players I work with, I can say my baseball career did not take an entirely traditional path. I started playing baseball at five years old because my dad was a baseball player. Where I grew up in Vernon, B.C., Canada, there was no high school or college baseball in the area, so I played club ball. I didn't pursue college baseball mostly because I didn't even know how to go about it and from an economic standpoint, living in my parents' basement while studying locally and continuing to play club ball made sense at the time. In hindsight, I wish I had had that baseball college experience to see what I could have made of it.

David Burns hits another bomb!

I came to Austria in 1999 as an import baseball player. A friend of mine connected with the club here via the Internet (yes, they had

Internet then), and recruited me to come be their power hitter. That was the end of my international baseball travel experience because I met, married and had children with a local Austrian woman. After four years of living in Canada with my new wife and then young family of two children, I returned to Austria permanently in 2005, restarting my baseball career and living in Salzburg. I have played ever since, from 2005 to 2017 in the Austrian Bundesliga, and today I continue to play on the second team with my son and plan to make a comeback to play with him in 2020 as he is promoted to the top division.

In terms of lessons learned from the game, my baseball career is also very unusual. The bulk of the lessons I learned have been since my return to Austria in 2005 at the age of 29 through now at the age of 45. Where I grew up in Canada, the opportunities in baseball weren't what they are today. I didn't have the coaching, and my dad, although a standout pitcher in the province of Ontario, never played college or professional baseball and never learned all aspects of the game on a deeper level to pass on to me.

Fortunately, over the years our club here in Austria has brought over many import players and coaches with college and professional backgrounds. All of these players brought a different perspective, different philosophy and new tidbits of information about our complex game. I had the raw skills and talent, but never truly started reaching some of my potential as a baseball player until my 30s. My best seasons as a baseball player came in my late

30s. And even into my early 40s, I was able to compete at a level almost as high as the imports across the Baseball League Austria.

With all that being said, as a player I never had the pressure that comes with the goal of being recruiting by a big athletic Division I or D1 school or getting drafted, so I simply just played because I love the game, love the camaraderie and love to compete.

As a result, from a mental standpoint, it is hard for me to relate to those who did have those goals, but I can say that I used to put a tremendous amount of pressure on myself to be "the guy" after being a standout in my hometown as a kid. Throughout my career I would fall into slumps because I was trying too hard to be "the guy." I would say it wasn't until about my mid-30s that I finally stepped back and looked at the big picture, that being "the guy" wasn't what it was all about and that being "with the guys" on the ball field having fun while competing together for a common goal was what it actually was all about. Once I made that mental connection, baseball has been the most fun it has ever been and my performance on the field has followed suit.

I can teach this lesson to many players who come to me looking to play overseas, whether college or professional, and often come with a bit of a chip on their shoulders because they feel like they have not been given a fair shake by professional baseball. Some of these players who come overseas feel they are too good for the level and then lose their work ethic and in turn don't produce, eventually hanging them up with a bitter taste on their career. However, most find it as a refresher to rediscover why they put a glove on in the first place back when they were a kid. So, what I have learned in my unusual baseball career is that until you can find that peace with the game and keep the big picture in mind, it doesn't matter how hard you work, you will not achieve your goal.

Because I adopted this mindset, the team and I have a number of achievements that I can talk about, but I think the best individual and team achievement are in the same story in 2017, when we were not expected to win the Baseball League Austria championship. We did, and I had my career moment on this journey.

During the Austrian championship series, we were up 1-0 in the series and down 6-1 in the bottom of the 5th in Game Two, one out with runners on second and third and our import clean-up hitter up to bat. They intentionally walked him to get to the 43-year-old slow guy (me). I took a 1-0 slider over the fence for a grand slam to make it 6-5. We ended up winning that game and eventually winning the series 4-3. It was extra sweet because at that moment, I felt confident I was going to win the way I have many times in the past. Ten years prior I would have choked (and did often). It was also extra sweet because of my age. I was the head coach, and this was my team, so I wanted to step up and motivate the guys and show them (and my kids who were watching) that the old fart still has it.

Many of you may be thinking right now while reading this, that this was "just" Austrian baseball, a level that you can compare to a low-mid D3 level. However, for me, it was a nice punctuation to the end of a 38-year baseball career, with a lot of memories and stories that

I will be reminiscing with my teammates for years to come and telling my grandkids in the future. So, for me, it was a great moment. It didn't have to come in the College or MLB World Series. And my dad watched that grand slam in the Austrian championship!

If there is ever a father that should be recognized for supporting his son in a productive, non-pressure way, it was my dad. He is 82 years old today and still my biggest fan and supporter. He religiously gets up at 5 a.m. to watch our games over here in Europe on the livestream. He is a big part of why I have continued into my 40s and why I have developed into the coach I am today. He was my coach for most of my youth, and although sometimes I didn't show my appreciation when I was a kid, it was something I wouldn't have changed for the world. I will always model my approach to coaching on his, which is a fun + intensity + high rep efficiency model.

My dad easily is the biggest impact, but there have been many

imports (and Austrian teammates) over the years who left their mark in one way or another and to try and name them all would be too much ,and I would be afraid to leave someone out. However, in most recent years the biggest impact came from import player (and coach) David Brandt in 2016 and 2017. He taught me to run the bases. As a result, I swiped an extra bag on a routine single and lazy outfielder or OF approach in the 2017 semis. This is something I had never done and to do it as a 43-year-old, 6'6" first baseman or 1B was pretty cool. He also helped me to find more power in an aging swing! This is I still demonstrate to the players who sign on with Baseball Jobs Overseas.

Burns goes yard....again!

Chapter 3

Emotional Intelligence by Scott Weaver and Coach Eric "Lefty" Niesen (USA)

By Scott Weaver and Coach Eric "Lefty" Niesen (USA)

As a pilot, pitcher and a coach with over 50+ years of experience, I felt like I had an interesting perspective on the game. I met Eric Niesen, former New York Mets and pitching coach for Georgetown University in 2018. He and I put together some thoughts for both players and coaches, geared towards the mental side of the game.

The Fighter Pilot's mental view of pitching comes from Lt. Col. Scott "Hurler" Weaver. The Coach's perspective on the physical side to pitching comes from Coach Eric Niesen, pitching coach at Georgetown University.

The Mental (Pilot's) View. Cool under pressure, systematic thinking and mental toughness – these are some of the characteristics you'll find in a fighter pilot and a pitcher! I should know. I'm a fighter pilot by trade with experience in both playing and coaching baseball. A strange combination, I know.

I have two major passions in my life besides my family: aviation and baseball. As you've read, as an Air Force pilot, I flew the T-

38A and F-16C. I was a combat-tested fighter pilot, instructor and evaluator during my long career with the USAF, and a solid baseball player. While the Los Angeles Dodgers and the Cincinnati Reds expressed interest in me during high school days, I instead signed with the legendary Coach Irv Brown at the University of Colorado as a pitcher. I played, coached, managed and scouted baseball for another 20+ years, while enjoying my career in the Air Force.

The Coaching View. Eric Niesen joined Georgetown University's baseball coaching staff in July 2017.

Niesen comes to the Hilltop after spending the 2017 season as a student assistant coach for the Wake Forest Demon Deacons. While completing his degree in communications, Eric assisted the Wake Forest pitching staff and served as the bullpen coach for the team under Georgetown alumna, Tom Walter.

Prior to his student days at Wake Forest, Niesen had a 10-year professional baseball career, reaching the Triple-A league with the Mets, Mariners and Red Sox organizations, as well as independent ball. He was a third-round draft pick of the New York Mets in 2007.

In the minor leagues from 2007-13, Niesen pitched in more than 150 games. He won 21 games and had a 4.51 ERA. Eric spent parts of five seasons in the Atlantic League, owning a 0.93 ERA with the Bridgeport Bluefish in 2015, his last full season. The New Boston, Michigan native stepped away from baseball during the 2016 season to be with his wife, Tina, as the couple had their first son, Gideon, now 4 years old and their daughter Casey Rae who will turn 2 years old next month. Strategic Combination.

Eric and I enjoy unique perspectives on the game of baseball and on pitching in particular. We've teamed up to write about the Fighter Pilot's Guide to Pitching. Our articles will include up-to-date pitching techniques culled from our unique careers. We'll provide insight from a former professional player and current Division 1 pitching coach and in combination, examine the mindset and mentality of a fighter pilot and how that mindset relates to baseball. When we talk about the relationship between pitching baseball and flying fighter jets, we'll provide a practical and experienced viewpoint – a winning combination for anyone who strives to be a better pitcher or better coach.

Emotional intelligence, or the capacity to control one's emotions prior to flying into "bad guy" territory, is not learned in one day. It takes years. It takes practice. It takes maturity. Emotional intelligence is the ability to self-manage. Being self-aware allows a person to have more control over their emotions, thereby creating a positive impact on themselves and the people around them. By guiding our own thinking and behavior, it's more likely we can perform at a high level. Being at that level, "in the zone," is something every elite athlete has felt at one time or another. To get into that zone, know yourself. Knowing your strengths, but more importantly, knowing your weaknesses is just as important whether you're climbing the bump or heading into combat.

Eric. I was drafted in 2007 out of Wake Forest University by the New York Mets - a childhood dream of mine following a decade plus of hard work. Throughout high school and college, I was also told I was too small to compete at the next level. Now I had the chance to prove those naysayers wrong. In my mind I had the tools, but did I have the emotional intelligence? Was I mentally prepared for the next level?

The next few weeks were a whirlwind of emotion. Your collegiate career ends coupled with the excitement of getting drafted. Now I was off to my first professional team, which sent me directly to Short-Season A ball in Brooklyn, NY. You would think the hardest part of that journey was dealing with the big city. In truth, the big city was just the beginning of the adventure. You are away from home and away from people you trust. You're thrust into a new environment - where every peer around you either wants your job or wants to get ahead of you. The difficult thing is the emotional toll of everything new - new coaches, new players, new city, new sleeping arrangements, long bus rides, distance from loved ones and the constant pressure to succeed. It was plain to me that if I was going to succeed at this level and higher, I had to develop a system to handle the mental side of the equation.

Scott. I started flying in the USAF in 1984 when I was selected to be a T-38 First Assignment Instructor Pilot (FAIP). In 1987, I transitioned to the F-16C. In all, I had twelve years of endless training to get ready for my first "combat" mission. How does 12 years of training prepare you for your first combat mission? How does that twelve years alter your level of emotional intelligence going into combat? Let me give you a couple of examples.

My first example recalls the feeling I had during the day of that first mission. It was reminiscent of my first start as a pitcher. I was pitching for University of Colorado as a freshman against the University of Oklahoma, a nationally ranked team at the time. I experienced a restless night of sleep, up early, with stomach turning, and an early arrival at the ballpark. Almost the exact same feelings I had at the start of this mission. Because there was a break in the action in Iraq, bullets and missiles weren't flying at the time. But the sense of readiness, preparedness, and emotional intelligence were similar. In both cases, I battled nerves but felt secure in the knowledge that I had been training for these missions my entire life.

Another more critical example of emotional intelligence during my flying days had to do with my first combat mission. It was in 1996 over Southern Iraq, flying out of Al Jabar, Kuwait. I was deployed with eight of my squadron mates and a maintenance, intelligence and weapons staff of over 50 personnel. Our mission was to replace an active-duty A-10 unit that had been stationed in the area for over a year. Our mission was primarily air-to-ground, carrying TV-guided Maverick missiles. At times, we would switch to a dedicated air-to-air role as we were ordered to look for "high fast flyers" – the Russian made Mig-29A coming out of Baghdad. Their mission was to defect or do serious damage to our High-Value Assets (HVA) like tankers or AWACS aircraft. Our mission was critical. We were mentally tough, aware of ourselves, motivated and emotionally intelligent.

Emotional Intelligence Learned. In the same way a professional pitcher has trained much of his young life to climb the mound and compete, ignoring the noise around him and focusing on the mission, so were we focused and confident. Two occupations. Two examples of real-world situations. Having the mental toughness, emotional intelligence, the body language, confidence and the attitude to go out and compete – the feeling is exactly the same, whether you're strapping on an F-16C loaded to the gills with weapons or meeting your highly anticipated competitor in a game where a large portion of the team's success depends on your skills and competence.

F-16C pilot checking his 6 O'clock

Whether it's bombs on target, or pounding the strike zone, having a process and experience dealing with factors outside of yourself, learning how to control your inner thoughts, is key to your success.

Despite the significance of emotional intelligence, its nature is intangible. It's hard to know exactly what qualities you have, or a potential colleague has, unless they are tested. Experience and practice are key to developing a high emotional intelligence.

Our next contributor is a good friend Coach Liam Carroll. Liam is a dual passport holder (US and UK), the former Head Coach for the Great Britain National Team US and recipient of most of the Copenhagen dip that traveled from the states!

Chapter 4

Contact Lenses of British Baseball by Liam Carroll (USA/UK)

Coach Liam Carroll. Head Coach GB National team

By Liam Carroll. Former Head Coach Great Britain National Team (US/UK)

Anyone who wears contact lenses knows that on some days, they just don't cooperate. One such day was my first with Great Britain Baseball, at a tryout for our U15 team in Croydon, South London, during the summer of 1996. A healthy dose of nervousness and the small rearview mirror of my mum's car didn't make it easy to put my lenses in. I finally joined the tryout and proceeded to airmail throws from shortstop (I'd not yet learned to aim for the belt) and let a grounder through my legs. Twenty-five years, more than a dozen countries visited, and myriad memories later, I guess there's a lot to be said for showing up, giving your best, and then giving your best again, no matter what your lenses are like.

My involvement in and love for baseball began with my dad. A native New Yorker who grew up a fanatical Brooklyn Dodgers fan, he eventually moved to London and met my mum, a teacher. Her jobs took us from London to Somerset and then to Bristol. In each place there was just enough baseball to keep the passion alive. In Somerset, Dad even started a team, the Crewkerne Cutters, and at twelve I was playing in a league for adults. He became involved with some of the key players in British Baseball, leading to that 1996 tryout that began my love affair with Great Britain Baseball.

I was able to play for our U15 and U18 national teams and made an appearance with our men's team at the 2003 European Championship where I was thoroughly out of my depth against the former (Erik Pappas) and future (Nick Markakis) Big Leaguers who helped Greece to a silver medal. And, as a Mets fan, I was in awe of Davey Johnson, who managed the Netherlands to the title. I followed in the footsteps of some British Baseball Hall of Famers by heading to California to play collegiate baseball, where my transition to coaching would begin.

Perhaps it was inevitable, considering family passions for baseball and education, that I would end up in coaching. I've served Great

Britain Baseball since 2004, as an assistant or head coach at the U12, U15, U18 and U23 levels. Since 2015 I've had the honor of managing our men's national team. And while my collegiate playing career was spent backing up middle infielders more talented than I, still, I was fortunate to spend some time at the NCAA Division 1 level, finishing my degree and spending five seasons on staff watching some incredible players at UNLV.

Baseball has taken me to Austria, the Bahamas, Belgium, Cuba, Czech Republic, France, Germany, Hungary, Ireland, Italy, Netherlands, Serbia, Slovakia, Spain, Sweden, Switzerland and the USA. Playing highlights include that '03 appearance at the European Championship and in the same year, my college team setting a then school-record for wins. And on the coaching side, winning the U18 European Championship Qualifier in 2004, a conference championship and NCAA tourney appearance in 2005, and reaching the final of the World Baseball Classic Qualifier in 2016, managing against the likes of Barry Larkin and Jerry Weinstein.

Chasing the wins certainly remains an important goal, especially at the international level. But just like my contact lens prescription has changed in order to have a healthy view of things, my perspective on baseball has evolved over the years. That's thanks to the most important opportunity my journey in baseball has provided: meeting and learning from empathetic and compassionate players and coaches who inspire action.

While British Baseball remains a small community, we've been fortunate to have welcomed some phenomenal coaches from around the world. One of the most influential on me was Vince Garcia, an "Envoy Coach" for Major League Baseball. Coach Garcia was tough but fair. He helped me become a sponge, to understand the importance of the details, and to appreciate that where there is flexibility within a framework, the very best of everyone on your team can shine.

Most importantly, the likes of Coach Garcia and other British Baseball mentors, such as my U18 head coaches Ian Smyth and Paul Vernon and heroes, such as British Baseball Hall of Famers Alex Malihoudis and Gavin Marshall (the only born and bred Brit to play professional baseball), taught me that we are in this together. The great baseball men and women I've met have understood that the best way for each of us to succeed individually is to succeed together.

This is the essence of baseball: that while the language, customs and style of play may be different, what we have in common is a desire to work together to achieve more. It's as constant as is ninety feet between the bases.

As we all know, baseball is a great vehicle to teach life lessons, perhaps the greatest. I think those lessons begin with "we over me." The more I've coached, however, the more I've come to appreciate that "different, together" is going to beat "same, together."

As a younger coach I was inclined to require uniqueness across the team (shave rule, for example) than to celebrate the uniqueness of every player. I think now that the best way for each of us to become the very best we can be and to achieve more is to celebrate the differences that everyone brings to the table.

The business of coaching is the business of citizenship. What we apply on the field our players will apply off the field. No one said it better than the legendary Augie Garrido: we are striving to help players find the confidence and courage to act on their ideas. Taking action of course being at the very core of elite citizenship. Whether it's in the minutiae of day-to-day life or in bold steps that change lives, elite citizenship requires action. This is something that's of course mirrored on the field: to execute a pitch, steal a base or make a play requires action. It's important therefore for coaches to provide opportunities for players to act. You are simply wearing the wrong contact lenses if you view coaching as your chance to control anything and everything that your players do.

And so, empathy and compassion are critical, because they lead to action. Without empathy and compassion, "we over me" will always be a hanging breaking ball that gets crushed by selfishness, and selfish players will be selfish citizens. Changing lenses for a moment, I'm reminded of the incredible power of backwards design, which is fundamental to practice planning. We plan our practices by working back from the desired result, which is more effective than starting with an arbitrary step without thought for how it connects to the desired result.

For example, you'll see progressions everywhere in baseball training: hitters moving from the tee to soft toss to batting practice or BP; infielders moving from kneeling partner drills to rolled groundballs to fungos (fly balls thrown for practice). These progressions are born out of backwards design: if the goal is Z, we have to figure out a suitable Y, a suitable X, and so on.

We can simplify and improve many areas of life by incorporating backwards design, and the journey to action is no exception. It's how empathy and compassion enter the equation, and it's inextricably tied to "we over me."

Have a think about the type of action you want to see from players: great team spirit; communication between pitches; seamless double plays and cuts and relays; supporting each other after mistakes and celebrating each other's successes. All of these actions require players to know, trust and care for each other. Action will follow when players understand each other deeply, and so it is that we arrive at the importance of coaches focusing on empathy and compassion as much as on Xs and Os.

Because of that focus, I'm forever an advocate for players and coaches travelling the world because the experiences will force upon you new perspectives. Why is having an adaptable perspective important? Because you'll never develop empathy or compassion without being able to adapt your perspective.

Throughout my travels I've been fortunate to learn from empathetic and compassionate leaders who inspire action. One such person is

Scott Weaver, who never fails to contribute to the players, coaches and teams he finds along his travels. As do all of the greats I've met, Scott pulls people up to help them achieve more, on and off the field.

Coach Carroll leading his team to the World Baseball Classic.

My next contributor is my son, who I'm so proud of, for his "Rise and Grind" approach to life. Keep up the fight!

Chapter 5

Ball & Glove - First Trip to Rotterdam by Jo Weaver (USA/France)

Jo Weaver interview with local French news network.

By Jo Weaver. French National Team (USA/France)

In the summer of 2002, I landed in Paris to play baseball overseas for the first time. I was fifteen years old and despite my young age, it was not my first time to Europe, as I had my French passport stamped a few times before. However, it was the first time I was traveling with my bat bag. I was there to play baseball for the French Junior National Team, and I had no idea what to expect. Apparently, there were baseball diamonds on the other side of the pond, but I had never seen one in France. However, I thought that if the mound was 60 feet 6 inches away, I was comfortable in any batters' box—my favorite place in the world. I had been playing baseball for as long as I could remember.

After a couple of brief rainy workouts in Paris, in front of a few key members of what they called the Federation of French Baseball, I was invited to partake in the European Championship in the Netherlands, which would take place later that summer. How did I get out to France in the first place, you may ask?

Easy. My dad is the one that first introduced me to the game. He and I share a lifelong love of baseball. One day, he typed in a search: French + Baseball, a.k.a. a language I fluently spoke + something I was good at. By doing this, my dad opened up a whole continent, hundreds of contacts, and life lessons and experiences I could never have envisioned. Without his gentle push of encouragement, I would have stayed in the familiar comfort of my batters' box at home in Maryland. Instead, he gave me the opportunity to grow and see if my talents would translate over new horizons.

I stood out on the French Junior National Team. I did not know what was going on. Although I spoke fluent French and was no stranger to being in foreign countries, there was still a culture shock from one side of the Atlantic to the other, without a doubt. Regardless, I just came off playing with a Junior Olympic team in a tournament in Detroit with kids who were a year older than me that were throwing upper 80s, and any 33-inch bat in my hand felt like a nice ball point pen to a writing enthusiast.

My team and I played three preparation games in Holland the week before the tournament started. I felt we had a pretty decent squad. These kids were athletic, fast, and could hit. We scored versus some local club teams, and our pitchers never gave up more than three runs in a game. I was fighting for a starting spot on the squad.

Jo, Syb and Lianne at another FSB Classic.

This elite world of sports was something I had never experienced. Here we found ourselves in a big bus and a fancy hotel with access to five coaches, two doctors, and a physical therapist/masseuse. Meals were planned. It was a well-oiled machine with funding behind it, due to baseball being an Olympic sport at the time. We had bags, jerseys, new pants, workout gear, and off the field uniforms with the emblematic France logo when travelling. I was in hog heaven. Gone were the days of having our moms sew patches on our jerseys. Our first game in pool play was against Germany. After Germany, we would face Italy (perhaps tournament favorites with the Netherlands). We would then round it off with Russia. We had no scouting reports, only rumors about other teams.

I corresponded with my dad every other day via email from the cyber cafe in the hotel. On July 6, 2003, the day before the tournament, I wrote in my perfectly privileged snot-nosed 15- year-old fashion, "Turns out the Italians were staying in our hotel, and the Russians show up tonight. I'm sealed as the right fielder for the team batting 7th or 8th. We visited the beautiful town of Zoetemeer. Beautiful European vibe but a li'l cold for my liking."

Our head coach was a Cuban defector who made his way to the island of Sardinia off the west coast of Italy where he coached baseball. He found his way to France a few years later where he married a French lady and started a family. He then became our fearless leader at the helm of the Junior National Squad. He was built like a house, a caramel tone to his skin, 5'7, high energy, fungo bat (a long, thin bat used for hitting a fly ball thrown for practice) seemingly glued to his hand, and he was a catalyst. This guy spoke Spanish, Italian, and French all at once. I hardly ever understood him. I would have to ask teammates to translate to French during debriefs.

Anyway, we were behind 0-2 in the second inning against Deutschland in the predicted eight hole. I battled back to a full count, assumed a fastball was coming again, and hit a frozen rope (a hard-hit baseball that flies in a straight line much like a rope that is frozen in a straight line) over the centerfielder's head for a triple. Easy game. Second time up, I led off and Coach Gerrado shouted with his hands cupping his mouth, *"Arribe la primer base,"* meaning, "Let's get this rally started," in French. For once his words were not lost in translation. First pitch, I laid a perfect drag bunt down third base line, no throw was even made. I could feel my bench was not enthusiastic like the triple, but more appreciative of the chess-like move as I high fived the first base coach.

The next day, I wrote back to Daddio saying, "The Germans jacked the ball, our pitchers are weak. I did a bullpen yesterday and did great, so they said I'm in the rotation. Germans cheer like a girls' softball team too, more details later..."

Something didn't add up, however. These were the best 17 and 18-year-olds in Europe. I had a good game and was seeing the ball well, but no one was touching upper 80 MPH like I had seen on my travel team from Maryland. What threw me off was on the offensive side of the ball, these guys had everything necessary for a deep run. Anthony Cross, our three-hole hitter, finished with the Best Hitter award and he was not the only one that could swing. Yet they completely gave up after being down a few runs. What we called "showing signs" in the U.S., i.e., signaling fatigue, disappointment, and dwelling on mistakes. In a silly game where failure is just common currency, these fellas had not failed enough. They had not pulled up their bootstraps as many times and when they did, they did not do it with ease. Strong opponents feast on that, and it is contagious to your teammates.

It is a great game, it's rumbling, I learned my strengths and weaknesses. The team were passionate people who appreciated my approach and wanted me to improve.

Jo Weaver at the University of Maryland.

Chapter 6

Rise and Grind by Scott Weaver and Eric "Lefty" Niesen (USA)

By Lt. Col. Scott "Hurler" Weaver and Coach Eric "Lefty" Niesen

Scott. I just downloaded the book written by Raymond John titled "Rise and Grind." I wish I had coined the phrase because it's something I aspire to every day when I get up. But I would add: Rise and Grind with a passion!

I truly started to understand the phrase "Rise and Grind with a passion" when I was a young lieutenant in the USAF. I'd been selected to return to Vance AFB, Enid OK, as a T-38 First Assignment Instructor Pilot or T-38 FAIP. To be selected as a FAIP was an honor. To fly the T-38 as an instructor is a dream. The jet was the first supersonic trainer. It had been around the block for several decades, but you could call it the "sports car" of a jet. It had tandem seats – with the Undergraduate Pilot Training (UPT) cadet in the front seat, and the Instructor Pilot (IP) in the back seat. I often refer to my three years as a FAIP as an extension of UPT. Or I tell people, "It took me four years to finish pilot training – 1 year as a student and 3 years as an IP." Moving from one side of the table as a second lieutenant (2LT) and "stud" or student, to the other side as a first lieutenant (1LT) and instructor pilot quickly became a grind.

F-16C wingman support if vital.

In pilot training, Rise and Grind meant getting up every day and flying one to three sorties of flights a day. You had to have that passion to make yourself a better instructor pilot, knowing you're helping train the best pilots in the USAF. Every 5 1/2 months we'd get a new class and recycle the entire program again. We'd switch each week from "early to late" start, meaning one week we'd have a 0600 report then the next week shift to a 0900 report.

While the schedule became a grind, I had a passion to fly and to instruct. It was hard work, but rewarding, especially knowing that I helped craft young men and women into the future pilots and leaders of the USAF.

Eric. That phrase "Rise and Grind with a passion" is equally pertinent to ballplayers. When it comes to recruiting ballplayers, we look for the prospective recruit who has a passion and love for the game. While each player is slightly different, once a player buys into the "Rise and Grind" system, we know we'll get the most out of that player. While their natural talent got them this far, our job is to work with them to achieve their maximum potential.

As a ballplayer who wanted to be as successful as possible, the Rise and Grind was real. I was always told I was too small to play or pitch at a higher level. That comment made me dig down even deeper. It was up to me to dispel that theory. I worked on it constantly. You can't just have that chip on your shoulder during a game, but you need that incentive almost daily – during workouts, practice sessions and when rising and grinding every day.

Lefty during his college years at Wake Forest.

To be clear, just to say "Rise and Grind" every day doesn't always work. There are no set methods or "cookie-cutter" programs that we force on our players to make them excel at what they do. Getting up at 0600 to work out won't make you a better baseball player, but working out smarter, whenever it's best for you, might be a more successful program.

Beyond Rise and Grind

Rise and Grind by itself is not enough. You have to have goals and an unwavering passion. We tell our recruits to push their body's limits – perhaps limits they've never experienced before. We tell them to take advantage of their opportunity here – not only as a player, but as a student. Once an athlete starts seeing progress – like a faster pitch, better flexibility and increased strength, they realize the Rise and Grind is worth it.

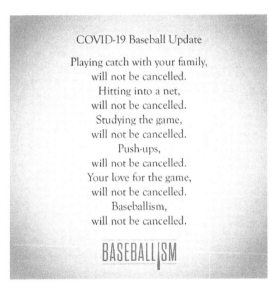

Covid-19 Baseballism. Author unknown

South America: Journeys from Buenos Aires International Airport (EZE), Argentina

Chapter 7

The Buenos Aires Shankees or "Yankees" by Scott Weaver (USA)

One of my first games with the Buenos Aires Shankees.

By Scott "Hurler" Weaver (USA)

After my first trip to Europe on the 777, and my first trip to London, I really became intrigued about where they were playing baseball around the world. American Airlines had flights from JFK to Buenos Aires. So, without hesitation I immediately typed into the "Google machine" baseball and Buenos Aires. Immediately the Buenos Aires Shankees popped up and the name... Paul Perry. The Shankees, a baseball team organized by writer/baseball player Paul Perry, were part of a league that played against the Dominicans, the Cubans, the

Japanese and some local Argentinians, and a lot of American expats. A lot of expats in Buenos Aires have left their homelands because of economic problems. There are a lot of Venezuelans, Dominicans and Cubans. The Japanese fled after WWII and came to Buenos Aires, plus thousands of Italians, and Germans, so it's a really pronounced international mix. Many of these people brought their love for baseball to Buenos Aires. Something we had in common!

I reached out to Paul. I said, "Hey Paul, you don't know me but I'm a pilot with American Airlines and I'm coming to Buenos Aires. What do you need? Can I bring you anything? Any chance I can play?" Paul was a character and excited about showing me what he had started in Buenos Aires.

I arrived Buenos Aires on a Saturday. The city's absolutely gorgeous. Many call it the "Paris of South America" because the design and architecture of many of the buildings are similar to those in Paris. When I first arrived there, the Shankees were playing at a stadium field near the Buenos Aires international airport (EZE), thirty minutes from my hotel. The stadium was built by the military back in the 1970s and early 1980s and seats about three or four thousand. Paul Perry was there at the stadium. Paul is this gregarious hippie-looking guy, full beard, glasses. "Hey dude!" He reminds me of a California surfer, but with a Philly accent.

I expected a normal handshake from the guy, but I instead got the Argentinian kiss on both cheeks like the Europeans or the French. Next, Paul called the Shankees (Spanish for Yankees) team together for a pregame meeting. It was a hodgepodge team, a recreational league level of play with high school and some college caliber players.

Paul handed me a soccer jersey, with a hand-painted logo of an "S" on it which stood for Shankees. It seemed it was Paul's ambition to create a baseball cult following for the Shankees.

We played on a baseball diamond that was scratched out of the corner of a soccer field. Paul somehow got a local politician to let him develop a baseball field at an abandoned park.

The game started and Paul didn't put me in right away, how could he? I was this random "dude" who had just flown an 8+ hours from JFK to Buenos Aires, working on a few hours' sleep and now was in a Shankees uniform in the middle of BA! After the third inning when our pitcher, from Boston, couldn't locate the strike zone and had walked the bases loaded, I waved to Paul. "Hey Paul, make a change, put me in," I said confidently. Paul, in his frustration with his starting pitcher, thought, "What do I have to lose?"

Sure enough, he put me in my first game in Argentina. He hadn't seen me play, but again, nothing to lose. I was running on fumes....two hours' sleep, jacked up on coffee, adrenaline and anxious to be in the game. The competitive juices started to flow.

The mound I was pitching on was made of plywood and torn up carpet. My catcher was from Venezuela and spoke very little English. But that was not a problem. The first batter out on three pitches—all fastballs. I was pumped. The guys in the field started chirping. "All right. Let's play some baseball," in both English and Spanish. The second batter came up. Same results. I struck out the second batter and two fastballs and a slider. This is fun!

I've pitched and played baseball now for over thirty years, and rarely have I seen a two batter strike out on six pitches. Both teams stopped and were all focused on the next batter. The Shankees dugout were all up and standing, clapping and starting to scream at the top of their lungs. I heard Paul say, "Oh my God, we've got ourselves a pitcher" in English and Argentinian Spanish.

I was still pumped up on adrenaline as the next batter stepped into the box. I started to get it into my own head: *Can I strike the third guy out in three pitches?* I stepped off the mound and took a deep breath to control my nerves. I reminded myself of the lesson I've taught my young players for the past decade. "One pitch at a time…one pitch at a time."

The Dominicans were a noisy team with lots of chirping and talk from the dugout. They were trying to get into my head, but I didn't hear it and I only focused on my target: the catcher's glove. Their "clean-up" hitter had a clue on how to swing the bat. The catcher put down the sign for a fastball, which had been the "go to pitch" so far. Knowing the hitter was thinking "dead red" fastball, I shook off my catcher and called for the slider which was working. Focus and execute. Focus and execute. First pitch, right on the corner, called strike one! The hitter was fooled as he was looking for some heat. Without delay or too much over thinking, I climbed the rickety wooden mound and quickly delivered the second pitch. He didn't miss by much! The guy had a huge swing, but just on top, and missed at a slider for strike number two.

Now it got interesting and I was in my own head. Just a few hours ago I had left JFK flying a 500,000-pound Boeing 777-200 down the coast of the Atlantic, through the middle of the Amazon and a sunrise arrival at 0700 into Buenos Aires. The noise from both teams was real and it was loud.

I stepped off the back of the mound and grabbed some dirt in my hands to rub up the ball. Guys in the field and dugout were pumping their fist and saying, "You can do this, you've got this!"

Granted it wasn't the World Series, but I finally took the time to acknowledge that I was doing something not many people have had a chance to do in their lives. I wasn't thinking of striking out the side, but I was thinking about playing the game I love in, of all places, Buenos Aires, Argentina.

I took a quick look around. The bases were still loaded just as they were a mere eight pitches ago. I took another deep breath to calm my nerves.

For the ninth pitch I was thinking "off speed" but shook off my catcher until he came back to the signal for the fastball. I knew this pitch should be off the plate, something he couldn't hammer. I took my windup and delivered the pitch and hit the target as I imagined it in my head and as my catcher had located his glove. Low and away. The pitch was beautiful! It was a pitcher's pitch…on the black, low and away and unhittable.

The umpire made what appeared to be his "called third strike" but instead quietly, almost to himself, said, "Ball." The Shankees dugout started to boo as the Dominicans dugout rejoiced. I quickly delivered the tenth pitch. Slider away and as it catches the corner of plate. Strike three! I struck a guy out, slider right at the knees, and the place went nuts.

Later in the game, when I reached first base, and the Dominican first baseman asked me in Spanish where I was from. I could speak a little broken Spanish and I managed to say, "I'm from Nueva York."

He said, "Nueva York? Well, when did you get into town?"

"Well, I got into town this morning."

"This morning?"

I said, "Yeah, I just flew in from New York this morning, and here I am playing baseball."

"Well, how long are you going to be in town for?"

I replied, "I'm going back tomorrow night. I'm only in town for thirty hours."

"What? You just flew down from New York for the day?"

"Yeah, it's a long story."

We ended up winning the game, and both teams celebrated by drinking beer, which is customary after all games in Argentina. We drank beer, reminisced about the game, exchanged stories, emails and got to know each other a bit better.

The umpire came up after the game, almost apologetic about not calling the ninth pitch a strike. He was an Argentinian who had never played the game, but only studied it online. His dream was to travel to Florida and attend an umpire's school camp to help develop his skills and the game he learned to enjoy from behind the plate. We struck up a friendship that day and remain friends today.

And I said, "You know that pitch I threw, that ninth pitch was on the "black," it was on the edge, you could easily have called that strike three."

He said, "Ah, Hurler, in my mind, it was a little outside," and we later laughed about it.

That was my first impression of the Shankees and their ragtag militia of passionate ballplayers and manager Paul Perry. I loved meeting these guys and continue to be friends with many of them today.

Scott and Paul Perry after a Shankee win.

Golden Lincoln Town Car.

My friend "Fast" Freddie from Texas runs a limo service or taxi service in Buenos Aires. He drives a Lincoln Town Car. It's probably the only Lincoln Town Car in all of Buenos Aires, let alone probably in all of Argentina. Even more extraordinary, it's a gold Lincoln Town Car.

He runs a limo service exclusively for people who are coming from the States or Europe, running business folks from Ezeiza, the airport, to downtown Buenos Aires and back. He, like a lot of expats, migrated to the Shankees because of the baseball. Freddie had never played baseball, but he's really intrigued about the game and was always asking about the rules and history. We became instant friends.

One time when I played a game in Buenos Aires, as per the norm, I flew all night from JFK. Freddie and his limo service offered to take me from the Ezeiza airport to wherever the game was. As it turned out, he ended up taking me back to field near the airport. I changed into my uniform at the Intercontinental Hotel in downtown Buenos Aires and I got back into Freddie's waiting gold Lincoln Town car. Fast Freddie was ahead of Uber and Lyft back then, because he had bottles of water in the back of the car.

I said, "Do you want me to sit up in the front with you?"

He said, "Scott, no, just sit back there in the back, you'll be more comfortable back." I sat in the back seat of the limo not thinking much of it and enjoying the view. As we approached the stadium, there was a side gate and a little dirt road that takes you back to where the field is.

Few can afford to drive a car in Buenos Aires. You have to be upper middle class to be able to afford to buy the car, let alone the gas and the insurance. So, when Freddie pulled up in his gold Lincoln Town Car, it attracted a lot of attention. It's a beautiful car, probably 1980s, so it's got old classic lines to it.

As we drove to the stadium, other games were going on. There were actually a couple of other fields and dozens of people watching Freddy's Lincoln Town Car as it came up. And I didn't think anything of it. We were playing the Cubans today at the stadium field, so my mind was starting to shift to the game.

I thanked Freddie, game him a $20 for the gas to run me out to stadiums. He dropped me off in front, where there was a game still going on, and sixty people were outside. Here I was rolling up in a Lincoln Town Car, with my uniform on. I got out of the back seat with a gym bag, cleats and glove and of course some new baseballs and some cans of dip.

As I got out and I opened the door, people stopped and watched me come into the stadium after getting dropped off by Freddy, and I didn't think anything of it. But to the few folks that were watching this beautiful Gold Town Car arrive, it looked like I was the "Lionel Messi" of Buenos Aires baseball, getting dropped off to help the Shankees. Thanks, Fast Freddie for your continued friendship.

In this section you will meet Paul Perry, but you will also meet: Chris Maloney, who I've known for 22 years ever since his father, and my best friend, "Uncle Mikey" Maloney, and I coached the youth baseball. Chris pitched in college and in Canada and was sent down on a standby pass to aid the Buenos Aires Shankees win their first championship title. You'll also meet my good friend, Pablo Tesouro, the Director of the Argentina Baseball League and well as Omar Prieto of Puerto Rico, who played as a catcher in the Argentina Baseball League as well as a club team in France.

Chapter 8

Outside the Comfort Zone by Chris Maloney (USA/Argentina)

Chris "Bud" Maloney- "No-Hitter" painted by Preston Sampson. 2011.

By Chris Maloney, Buenos Aires Shankees Import (USA/Argentina)

I started playing machine-pitch baseball for the Upper Montgomery Athletic Club when I was seven years old, which started a twenty-seven-year career in baseball that continues to this day. As a child, I had heard stories about my father playing baseball and would often attend his men's league games. Shortly after my first few games, I was having success and was instantly hooked. From that point on, I never had any interest in playing any sport other than baseball.

For both of my trips to Canada and Argentina, I was taken completely out of my comfort zone. I had never been out of the United States without familiar people at my side; however, I knew these trips playing baseball would provide me with lifelong memories.

In 2009, following my collegiate career and successful rehabilitation from Tommy John surgery to repair a ligament in my elbow (named for major league pitcher Tommy John, the first baseball player to undergo the procedure) at my college, Embry Riddle, where I played for the Eagles (including in three NAIA World Series, now NCAA Division II World Series) in Daytona Beach, Florida, I was given the opportunity to pitch for the Swift Current Indians (now the Swift Current 57s). I was not familiar with the Western Canadian Baseball League (WCBL) and had never been to Canada, but I was excited at the thought of giving it one more go after a major reconstructive arm surgery.

Initially, I had mixed feelings joining the team. The Indians were one of the top teams in the WCBL and had several members of the team who had played together for a few seasons. While excited to join one of the league's top teams, I was worried about the time in which the close-knit group of players would accept a new member to their team. After only a few days of pre-season practice and nightly outings with the players, I was accepted as one of the Indians. General Manager and Head Coach Joe Carnahan helped create an excellent "team" environment where every player was valued and respected.

I was grateful for the chance to play for the Indians and enjoyed my time meeting teammates from all over North America.

A Shankees From Day One

Almost ten years later in May 2017, I was approached by Buenos Aires Shankees Player Recruiter/Sponsor (and author of this book!) Scott Weaver with an offer to travel to Argentina for the weekend and play in the league championship game. Initially I thought the idea was crazy. I had been playing men's league baseball leading up to the offer, but to me, traveling to Buenos Aires for the weekend with only a few days' notice was out of the question. However, thanks to Scott reassuring me that all the travel and housing arrangements would go smoothly, I agreed without thinking much more about it. I found myself in a similar situation to my Canada trip, nervous and extremely out of my comfort zone. Less than two days later, I was flying out of Washington, D.C. to LaGuardia, catching a bus across the city to JFK, and boarding another flight to Argentina. It was a travel day I would never forget, but well worth it after getting to experience Buenos Aires culture for a short weekend. Thanks to Scott being a pilot, he was able to get me on a few flights on last minute notice, traveling in style from JFK to Buenos Aires.

Arriving a day before the championship game, I met with Head Coach Jay Bartelli and a few players from the team. They immediately made me feel welcome and quickly eased my nerves of being in a foreign country, playing with an unknown group of men. Before I knew it, we were taking the team bus to Ezeiza Estadio de Beisbol and a few hours later the Shankees defeated the Cuban National Baseball Team 5-3. The celebration following the game was one that I will never forget as both teams were bonding and congratulating each other on a hard-fought season. Even though I was only a Shankees for nine innings, the players treated me as if I were with them from day one. The championship celebration continued into the early morning and after a few hours of sleep, my time in Argentina was over. I spent about the same time traveling as I did total in Buenos Aires, but it was an experience I would never forget.

My only regret was I wish I could have stayed longer. I thought to myself throughout the weekend journey that I would never such an opportunity again. I am incredibly grateful that I took the leap of faith and had the support of so many to help make it happen, especially Scott Weaver.

I've known Scott and his family for about 22 years. I was twelve when my father began coaching the Upper Midwest Athletic Conference All-Star travel team. Scott became the coach of the 11-year old team. From then on, Scott and my father have been best friends and have played on many men's league baseball teams together.

Scott had always been looking out for my baseball career, trying to get me hooked up with overseas teams. We were finally able to make it happen when I went to Argentina to play for the Shankees.

My biggest takeaway from my baseball adventures outside of the U.S.? The often-overlooked ability to get along with teammates. While traveling twice outside of my comfort zone, I was welcomed with open arms by two groups of players, coaches and families. For those of you who read this, thank you.

Lessons of a Life in Baseball

The lessons learned from the game of baseball have helped me become the person I am today. Most importantly, hard work, and what you put in is what you get. I can say to this day that I still apply that simple yet impactful motto to anything I do in my everyday life. Other lessons:

Goal Setting

Goal setting was a particularly important part of my playing career and an aspect of the game that I adopted during my travel baseball years. Every year during "Winter Workouts," I would write a list of individual and team goals that I had hoped to accomplish during the upcoming spring and summer seasons. Having these goals with me always helped motivate me during a difficult run or late-night batting practice session at the batting cages. The goals provided me with a purpose and gave me the competitive fire that I still carry with me to this day.

When I moved on to high school and college, goal setting was still part of my yearly preparation whether it was getting stronger at a certain lift in the gym or winning a certain number of games on the mound. As a coach, I have taken pride and joy in passing on my knowledge of the game and watching the development of boys as young as seven years old who set goals and dedicate themselves to grow into NCAA Division 1 college athletes and fine young men.

Mental Toughness

From childhood on, I struggled with my emotions while on the field. I wanted to be perfect at every aspect of the game. Whether it was at the plate or on the mound, if things did not go my way, I would let it affect how I continued to play. It was not until my freshman year of college at Embry-Riddle that I understood the concept of mental toughness. My college coaches continuously pushed the idea of mental toughness and being able to push past failures, whether mental or physical, by remaining positive and competitive. I learned how to prepare myself to be mentally ready for any challenge and by my sophomore year, I was unfazed by any "failure" on the field. If I did not execute a pitch or an error was committed behind me, I learned to reset and conquer the next challenge. My confidence was at an all-time high, and that translated to individual and team success. Little did I know my coaches were preparing me for a life after baseball and how to handle adversity while being mentally tough.

Advice from Coaches

My college coaches Greg Guilliams and Randy Stegall taught me how to prepare for every outing on the mound, create a routine in between starts and hold myself accountable for executing every pitch. The reporting and scouting used before and after every game I pitched, truly helped me understand the art of pitching and how to set up hitters rather than just attempting to throw strikes. Learning these techniques helped me see the game from a different perspective, which in turn, created my desire and love of coaching, thanks to these coaches and the experiences they provided.

My Father's Lessons

As I sit here in front of a computer a week before Father's Day, it is hard for me to put into words the impact that my father, Big Mike Maloney, has had on me both playing and coaching baseball. Thinking about all the time we have spent together on the baseball diamond, so many memories come to my mind. The best way to elaborate on his impact would be to say thank you...

Thank you for:

- Introducing me to the game that I love
- Taking me to every Orioles-Mariners game to watch Ken Griffey Jr.
- Being my personal catcher and putting up with my wild arm before I found my accuracy
- Coaching every season from age 8 to 15

- Opening The Hitting Streak and providing me with the tools to succeed

- Throwing me hours of batting practice or BP, even though I critiqued every ball you threw out of the strike zone

- Keeping your distance when I did NOT want to be coached

- Working hard and teaching me that it takes hard work to achieve a dream—my dream of playing college baseball

- Being my voice of reason and motivation when I had doubts after my freshman year of college

- Flying across the country to watch me pitch in the NAIA World Series

- Meeting me at 5 a.m. every morning to lift weights during the Summer of 2006

- Saving every newspaper article

- Being one-half of the dominate Father-Son Baseball Classic tag team

- Being a great Assistant Coach when I took over the Caps

- Being right there with me when my arm was reconstructed (twice)

I could go on forever, but most importantly, whether it be in person, on the radio or through the computer, thank you for never missing a game.

Jo Weaver, Mike and Bud Maloney and Scott Weaver. 2019

Chapter 9

A Goal Without A Plan Is Just A Wish by Scott Weaver and Eric "Lefty" Niesen (USA)

By Lt. Col. Scott "Hurler" Weaver and Coach Eric "Lefty" Niesen

Most people would agree that setting goals is important. Without goals in life, work or sports, it's like having an airplane with no rudder. Well, maybe not that critical. Of course, it's a bit dramatic to give such an example since a plane without a rudder would crash. However, put another way, a boat without a rudder would just wander around aimlessly, without direction. In this article we'll discuss goal and objective setting for pilots and pitchers.

Scott. At one point in my career, I had ample time to reflect and decide what my next assignment would or could be. The needs of the USAF always took precedence over the individual's needs, of course, but I set my first long term goal of flying the F-16C - the super sleek, fly-by-wire, multi-role jet fighter.

I had never been trained on "goal setting" per se, but as a reminder of how I woke up to the "Rise and Grind" mentality, I saved a photo of the F-16C flying straight up into the blue sky. You see, the F-16C had what was called a "1 to 1 thrust to weight" ratio, meaning the jet weighs 30,000 pounds and the Pratt and Whitney engine could produce 30,000 pounds of thrust. It was the first generation of fighter jets that could climb straight up and maintain (for the most part) airspeed and continue to climb!

F-16C in full Afterburner

Eric. I decided on my assignment. I wasn't drafted out of high school, so my goal was to pitch for a top tier D-1 program. When Wake Forest University offered me the opportunity to pitch in Winston Salem, NC, I jumped at the chance. When I arrived on campus, I made my long-term goal to get drafted into the MLB. I knew I had to get stronger, faster and smarter. My smaller goals or objectives were all geared toward that ultimate goal of putting on a big-league uniform.

Today, I am a coach, helping students reach their dreams. Next week our coaching staff welcomes a new class of freshman to our campus. It's an exciting time for them as well as our coaching staff. Similar to the new recruits in the military, we'll introduce them to our baseball culture and our way of doing business at our university. Part of that is instilling the need for goal and objective setting. Not only do we talk about team goals, like winning championships, but we set more specific goals for our pitching staff. Then we take it a step further and discuss individual goals. We use leaderboards or spreadsheets to track such things as strike percentages, velocity and execution in the bullpen. We'll track different stats to create a competitive atmosphere amongst the pitchers, not by design, but by setting goals and objectives to make everyone on the staff better.

At a higher level of objective setting, we'll track pitch patterns or pitch combinations, such as: Fastball/curveball/fastball in different locations. If a pitcher can get through that combination of pitches, then we'll step up a level (leveling up) and challenge him with other combinations.

One of our team goals we set last year as a staff was K/9 innings – the number of strikeouts per nine innings. It's clear, concise and measurable. And it paid off big time! Last year we led the conference in that category which, as every coach and pitcher will tell you, is a key stat in any team's success.

And finally, we talk about how to win using reverse engineering. In other words, we look at successful teams and pitching staffs and analyze what they do to win. There's no point in measuring stats like exit velocity if it doesn't help us win. Bottom line, we're not trying to reinvent the wheel and come up with new or different concepts to pitching, but we want to have clear and concise goals and objectives that every player understands. Those goals and objectives need to do one thing and one thing only – help us win!

Scott. As a pilot with just under 2,000 hours in the F-16C, most of our missions or "sorties," were between 1 hour to 1 hour and 20 minutes long. Each training sortie had goals or objectives - such as bombs on time on target (BOTOT). Each goal was specific, measurable, attainable, relevant and timely (SMART). The over-arching goal of each mission was to prepare us for war. The objectives of each mission were the means to measure our direction to the final goal.

Championships celebrated

Eric. Although the goals and objectives of a coach are not life or death, it's my goal to push my athletes to their personal limits. While I'm not trying to make every student-athlete a professional ballplayer, my goal is to teach them to be a better person - in life, and on and off the field. I do this by sitting down with each player at the beginning of the season with the purpose of setting specific goals. And we discuss objectives on how to reach those goals. The more specific those goals are, the better. One goal we might have is: "Winning a Championship." Then, we set objectives on how to get there. Examples of these objectives might include:

- Throw first strike pitches 65% of the time.

- Develop a third pitch you're comfortable throwing at any time in the count.

Breaking the game down into smaller goals, giving players concrete examples of how to reach their goal, gives them direction. Otherwise, setting long term goals without objectives is kind of like the boat without a rudder!

Scott: Currently, I'm mentoring a cadet at the American Airlines Flying Cadet program.

2-ship of F-16C from the DC Air National Guard. 1990

Brandon, who is 20-something and from the Dallas, Texas area, wants to be an airline pilot. The requirements to become a commercial airline pilot are daunting. There are multiple exams, both written and oral.

There are dozens of check rides and evaluations and ratings to obtain –
from private, instrument, commercial, instructor to air transport
ratings. It's at least an 18- to 24-month program of hard work and
determination. From Brandon's perspective, the task is a huge
mountain to climb. Last week Brandon struggled with his first oral
exam on the subject of take-off and landing data. This week he asked
me for tips on how to flare the aircraft for landings – all basic bricks in
the foundation. His attitude is outstanding, but at times he seems
overwhelmed.

However, we have a plan to get Brandon to his dream job. We started
by breaking his long-term goal down into smaller objectives, just as
you heard from Eric. When I asked Brandon what his ultimate goal
was, he said, "To be in the right seat of a legacy airline, yanking the
gear handle of a Boeing 737 or an Airbus-320 and someday to fly the
Boeing 777-300."

I told Brandon to put the photo of the Boeing plane shown here on his
iPhone as his home screen or place it somewhere where he'll see it
daily. Together we have now solidified his ultimate goal to become a
commercial airline pilot. Everyday he'll move forward with smaller
tasks or objectives to help him accomplish his dream. His confidence
shows. "I'll do whatever it takes," was his response. Now, posting a
photo where he can see it day-in and day-out serves as his inspiration.
He'll have days, weeks and months of "Rising and Grinding" to meet
his true goal of being a commercial airline pilot – but he is well on his
way.

Not just for pilots and pitchers. In conclusion, setting goals and objectives are not only important in flying or baseball, but in all facets of business and personal life.

777-200 approach into London Heathrow. (LHR)

Moving toward success. If you're a coach, sit down with your players and give them some clear goals and objectives. This could be the first time they've actually thought about the concept of goal setting. If you're an aspiring pilot or someone who just wants to get better, stronger and smarter, set clear goals and objectives. Write them down so you can see them every day. The process helps give you a clearer sense of direction. Make sure they are clear, specific, measurable, attainable and timely goals, and most of all paint that picture in your head so you wake up and face the day-to-day challenges of succeeding!

Chapter 10

Godfather of Expat Baseball in Buenos Aires by Paul Perry, (USA/Argentina)

Paul Perry conducts a local interview in BA.

By Paul Perry, Founder of the Buenos Aires Shankees (USA/Argentina)

The final game of the 1976 Little League season at Capitolo Park (just off the 9th Street market in South Philadelphia) was the last time I played baseball in the States, and it wasn't until 2002 in Buenos Aires, Argentina that I would once again put on a glove, throw a ball, and swing a baseball bat in honor of my American roots, to share the beauty of this game with my two-year-old son, Henry, who would accompany me throughout my Shankees baseball days.

The Shankees dream began when, after running a Google search for baseball in Buenos Aires, I came across a man in white who ran a small baseball program from deep within a shady municipal park on the outskirts of the city. I immediately became a part of his Buenos Aires field of dreams by helping him develop the infrastructure, coach the kids he recruited from the adjacent shantytowns, and eventually form part of his weekend pick-up games. Most of the players were Cubans or Argies and I was obviously the only gringo or what they called "yanqui."

Despite not having played baseball for almost 25 years, I did grow up playing half ball, stickball, wiffleball, and understood the game from spending many summer afternoons in the 50- cent bleacher seats of Veterans Stadium. There was nothing like being at a baseball game in Philadelphia during the summer. My most memorable baseball moment growing up was when the Phillies won the World Series in 1980. We didn't have a TV, so my friends and I watched the final innings through the window on a neighbor's TV.

I wanted to bring that baseball excitement to Argentina. Unknowingly, the man in white and his precarious field prompted me to embark on a baseball ride that would lead me to revolutionize the game locally, as well as to fill thousands of expats from all walks of life with eternal memories of baseball in Buenos Aires.

The Birth of the Shankees

Father and son. Shankee Nation. 2012.

In the summer of 2008, the man in white decided to organize a tournament consisting of four teams: a team from Rosario City, a Cuban team, a Dominican team, and a Gringo (yanqui) team. I had met several expats over the years, and I felt confident I could field a team. Also, I knew where most of the expat community hung out, so I set out to recruit potential players. One night, while watching the Dodgers-Phillies division series at the Alamo together with John Harris, who played shortstop and was my catcher on Team America (05-07), we decided to start a team and enter the tournament.

Together with a few friends of friends, we fielded the first ever all-American expat baseball team in Buenos Aires. I named the team the Shankees, which combines the /SH/ pronunciation of Yanquis with the double EE of the Yankees. The Shankees went undefeated in the tournament and in 2008, entered the LMB (Liga

Metropolitana de Beisbol) for summer/fall season to become the first- ever all-American team to play baseball in Argentina.

Baseball in Soccer Country

Baseball gets no love in soccer country, but by 2009, I honestly believed that I could turn baseball into the top sport in Buenos Aires. Why? Because I felt that kids, as well as my son, deserved to experience the beauty of baseball through its discipline and the importance of teamwork. Plus, I wasn't a big fan of soccer and the violent aggression it represents in Argentina. Hence, I applied all my creativity, my American drive and passion, and my sporting moments at Veterans Stadium and the Spectrum to help create a successful baseball organization. Thus, I set out to target all U.S. expats studying or living in Buenos Aires for a dose of baseball.

My first ever post for baseball players was on Craigslist under *Activity Partners* and read: **PLAY BASEBALL IN BUENOS AIRES. PLAYERS WANTED. UNIFORMS AND GEAR PROVIDED!!**

Following that post, players popped up season after season and from all walks of life. During that first season, I created a Facebook page, developed a Website and had stickers made, which I stuck in bar bathrooms and handed out to anyone on the street that looked like a gringo. Our popularity within the local baseball community grew and after a few seasons, many of the other teams not only emulated the Shankees, but also yearned to play the Shankees, because playing against the Shankees would be the closest they would ever get to playing ball in the U.S.A. or in their favorite movie.

Despite all the enthusiasm, two of the biggest challenges I faced during my ten years running the Shankees were logistics and funding, but I thrived on conquering them. Thus, I made sure to secure funding to rent a bus to take the players, their friends, and baseball fans to the games. During the ride, I sold tickets to the games, hats, t-shirts and handmade pendants, raffled off autographed baseballs, and did whatever it took to cover costs, which included broken bats, lost balls, umpire fees, field rental, etc. Handling every aspect of running a baseball team made up of expats in Buenos Aires was a tremendous challenge that required focus and mental toughness, and sometimes I even had to pitch. However, promoting the team and baseball was what I did best. I wrote post-game recaps and posted team news, which I splattered all over social media.

Eventually, the Shankees became one of the most popular teams in Argentina, with their popularity spreading into Chile, Bolivia, Peru, the United States, and around the world. By 2010, the Shankees had created a youth team called the Shankees Juniors and we were enroute to domination. However, in Argentina kids didn't decide what sport they wanted to play, especially those with soccer-crazed dads. This was a sad fact that still makes the growth of baseball in Argentina a bust. Regardless, the Shankees reached their baseball pinnacle upon going undefeated in 2018 and winning the championship with a victory over the Cuban Expat team. The

Shankees dropped out of the league in 2019 after a failed season in the top division, but their legacy will live on forever. From 2008-2018, some 500 players from countries around the world played baseball for the Buenos Aires Shankees.

Let there be no doubt that baseball in Argentina would not be what it is today if not for Paul Perry, the Shankees players, its fans, and its supporters like Jason Hermes, Fast Freddie, and of course Scott Weaver.

The Pilot Pitches in Buenos Aires

I met Scott during the summer of 2011, three years after founding the Shankees.

Scott walked into the Shankees Clubhouse one cloudy summer morning and became that ray of sunshine that made the Shankees shine. I could tell right away that his interest in baseball was unique and true, especially after having spent over a decade in Argentine baseball and almost a lifetime among Argies or Argentinians. Thus, Scott and I immediately hit it off.

I'm sure he was able to see my drive and passion for the game, especially after showing him around my clubhouse and my field, which I had named Shankees Stadium. This was basically an abandoned softball field that had an equally abandoned clubhouse. I had been there for barely a month when Scott walked in, which by that time, I had managed to paint the interior red, white, and blue and filled it with baseball memorabilia...much of which came and went because of the threat of getting robbed when I wasn't there.

After all, Shankees Stadium was, ironically enough, right next to the field where my baseball daze had started, nestled amid the villas and with the man in white. But that is another story...

Scott eventually joined the team and his first appearance as a Shankees was most memorable because he had flown into B.A. that morning and said he would be able to play in the afternoon. I said, "Great."

One problem: I had not signed him up and the league always paid special attention to the players on the Shankees line-up and on the roster. What can I say? Word of my sneaky ways spread within the league and everyone had their eyes on the Shankees given our constant player turnover. Because my motto was simply, "if you're a gringo, get in there."

Thus, Scott Weaver took the game as Ryan Scott in his Shankees debut in a game against the all- Dominican team called the Cardenales, who suspected Scott was a ringer since word quickly spread that he literally flew in from NY to play for the Shankees. He was a dead-on ringer. The most memorable ringer in Shankees history!

Well, Scott continued to play for the Shankees sporadically whenever flying into B.A. and apart from becoming a part of the growth of the Shankees through his on/off the field skills, his passion led him to becoming a huge part of making sure the Shankees had the bare essentials to play the game in B.A. As time passed, Scott's interest and participation grew, as did the Shankees' influence on baseball in Buenos Aires and in Argentina as a whole.

I embarked on a youth baseball project to include local schools and Scott helped me to spread baseball within underprivileged communities by way of multiple contributions in terms of gear for both youth and adult baseball. In fact, thanks to Scott's efforts combined with my drive to spread the game, baseball began to appear throughout Argentina in places such as Rawson, San Luis, and other small cities. With Scott on board, the Shankees were taking to the heavens. In fact, and no pun intended, the Shankees made it all the way up to God.

Scott's effort reached the religious community after I put him in touch with a man named Mike Figi, whom I referred to as the Bizarro Shankees Skipper. I had met Mike at one of the weekly league meetings, which I usually attended after having a few beers during the drive over there.

When I met Mike, I asked him the same question people asked me upon making their acquaintance, *"¿Que haces acá?"* Which translates into, "What are you doing here?"

Because a gringo has to be nuts to live in Buenos Aires.

Mike's response was one that I would never forget: "God told me to come to Buenos Aires to teach baseball."

Thus, Mike took on God's command, left his hometown leaving his memorabilia shop behind and began teaching baseball to Argentine kids in the underprivileged communities as I focused on adult gringos living in the nicer neighborhoods. Mike was all about kids and righteousness, while I was all about adults and partying. Therefore, I nicknamed him the Bizarro Shankees Skipper.

I put Scott and Mike in contact when the latter received a huge donation of baseball gear from folks within the religious community in the States. The only problem was getting the gear from wherever it was in the states to Buenos Aires. Scott's efforts made Mike and God smile every time Scott would fly to B.A. with the donated gear in tow, bringing joy and the possibility of baseball to the kids that made up Mike's activities. Mike and I eventually joined forces to enhance our baseball expansion efforts, but God had other plans for me, since being all-knowing, he realized there was no way of mixing water and oil to make wine. After all, Mike Figi and the Aguilas were like the alternate universe Paul Perry and the Shankees—Mike and I were complete opposites.

Apart from becoming friends, we became partners in propelling the Shankees to the top. By 2018, the Shankees had put together one of the finest all-round baseball teams in the league and made Argentine baseball history by becoming the first-ever expat team to go undefeated and win the division championship. The Shankees no longer compete locally for reasons best left unsaid, but the Shankees Flame will burn forever within the hearts in the thousands of people from around the world who got a dose of Shankees Baseball in Buenos Aires, Argentina.

Paul Perry. US Expat. Buenos Aires, Argentina. 2015.

I met, our next contributor, Pablo Tesouro, in the Intercontinental Hotel lobby bar where he told me about his dream to start a professional baseball league in Northern Argentina. Talk about giving back to baseball! Pablo has put his passion and money and has Major League Baseball (MLB) interested in supporting his dream to quality baseball in South America.

Chapter 11

The Mental Approach by Scott Weaver and Eric "Lefty" Niesen

By Lt. Col. Scott "Hurler" Weaver and Coach Eric "Lefty" Niesen

There's a mental side to both occupations. As a fighter pilot, we rely on our wingman. He or she is there when we need support. The same goes for pitchers. They must rely on their wingmen – the catcher and his teammates – for defense and player insight. There's a certain psyche, a combination of intelligence, bulldog mentality, attitude and toughness that both jobs demand.

Owning the Pitch. Climbing the mound with mental toughness is the same attitude a fighter pilot takes when he climbs the ladder to strap into his jet. The mind is determined and confident, knowing he or she is prepared for the mission. In combat, as missiles are launched, a pilot must maintain her composure. A pilot learns to prioritize her actions to stay alive. Similarly, when a pitcher takes the mound, he embodies the same confidence and mechanics of a fighter pilot.

Max Scherzeer and his fighter pilot mind set.

The Development of Mental Toughness. Both professionals, fighter pilots and pitchers, approach their particular endeavors through a systematic strategy of consistent practice and planning. Success in a mission or on the field does not happen by accident. A thorough knowledge of the subject is critical when it comes to success and achievement. And perhaps even more important is keen mental preparation. While baseball may not be as forward-thinking as the military with regards to mental preparation and emotional control, still, the challenge is the same.

Preparing Pitchers. So, what does it take to build mental toughness in a pitcher? We make the training environment tough. We instill challenging drill work, promote vigorous practice that replicates real games, focus on mental training and practice breathing techniques. When a pitcher steps on the mound and the hitter stands in the box, there's a perception that one player is confident and ready to take advantage of the other. That's the purpose behind building mental toughness. You must KNOW you are better than the other guy – that you've trained well and know how to execute pitches or hit the ball in stressful conditions. Over time, winners are stronger both mentally and physically. In baseball, as in flying fighter jets, winning or losing generally comes down to a single moment. Be Ready.

Chapter 12

My Argentinian Baseball Story by Pablo Tesouro, (Argentina/USA)

Scott and Pablo Tesouro. Bethesda Big Train College Baseball. Bethesda, MD. 2019

It is impossible to answer the question, "What do you love about baseball?" There is no rational answer!

I do know that my love of the game has grown since the first time I played baseball with friends at the age of nine, encouraged by the father of a friend who had lived and played in the U.S. In 1994, at the age of 22, I was part of the Argentinian national team, Los Gauchos, that was getting ready to participate in the Pan American Games of 1995. The Pan American Games were a major moment in Argentinian baseball, and the country prepared for the games, as did my team. The process was very demanding, but it was an honor.

Unfortunately for me, things happened, and I was released from the team in December 1994, and quite disappointed with myself for not being able to play the Pan Am Games.

Meeting Pedro Martinez

Back in my hometown where I played baseball with several clubs, by coincidence, a visiting team from Monte Plata Dominican Republic came, and I had the chance to be seen by some of the coaches, who invited me to the Dominican Republic (DR) and made the connections for me to land in Campo Las Palmas Dodgers Training Camp. One day, our home team in Las Palmas was scheduled to play the Oakland As. Before the game, the coaches gave the lineup and I saw my name as designated hitter (DH), but to everyone's surprise they did not announce the starting pitcher.

All of a sudden, when we were getting ready for the warmup, a stunning red car showed up and Hall of Famer Pedro Martinez got out, already dressed in the Dodgers uniform. With him were Juan Guzman, the famous Blue Jays pitcher, and Pedro's brother Ramon Martinez, another big leaguer!

Pablo Tesouro and Pedro Martinez on a "Dodgers" uniform. February 1995 at "Campo Las Palmas" Dodgers training facility and Academy in Dominican Republic.

For some people it might be odd seeing Pedro wearing a Dodgers uniform in 1995, but he had very close friends on the team and it was the year of the strike. He happened to be in the Dominican Republic and needed a spot to stay sharp...what better and more private place than the Dodgers camp where he had old-time friends?

Pedro shook hands with all the players. He asked who the catcher was, and said, "Let´s do some bullpen game starting in a few minutes, right?"

We were all amazed to share six innings with Pedro that day. He was very friendly and humble, and all players respected him and his space. He was definitely one of us that day! After the game, we talked a lot about baseball and Argentina.

My experiences at the DR opened my eyes about what organized baseball was. Unfortunately, I was already 23 and too old to become a professional baseball player. Even though I was invited to stay in the Dominican Republic, I decided pro baseball was done for me and decided to go back to school to finish my degree in Clinical Biochemistry from the Universidad Nacional de Córdoba. I discovered the lessons of passion for the game, hard work and learning to be resilient, and applied the hard work and resilience to the biochemistry degree.

In 2000 I got accepted to Missouri State in Springfield, Missouri in the United States and enrolled to work on a Master of Business Administration. With time, dedication and hard work, I graduated at the top of the class with a 4.0 and I learned about semi-pro baseball and organized baseball leagues, and in the U.S., my love for baseball matured.

While in the U.S.A., every summer I played semiprofessional baseball in high-end semi pro leagues for the Ozark Generals and the Springfield Slashers in Missouri, the Mount Wolves in York, Pennsylvania, and the Phillies in Dallas, Texas. Playing in this environment in the U.S.A. helped me to understand the game better. It was the best time of my life and I really enjoyed the game. It also helped me understand professional and semi-professional organizations and get a lot of ideas and advice.

All these experiences along with my experience playing semi pro ball in the US and being able to study my MBA in Missouri hanging around a lot of baseball buddies certainly helped me to plant the seed of the future Argentina Baseball League.

I had contacts with people from Las Palmas such as Pablo Peguero, the former head of operations with Estrellas Orientales and a very well-known baseball person in DR and with the San Francisco Giants (he left the Dodgers some years ago), also with my buddies in Missouri. I still have strong friendships with these people. I consult with them on almost every important project I do and get incredible help and ideas every time. Their support and knowledge were invaluable when I decided to create the Liga Argentina de Baseball (LAB) in 2017.

The Argentina Baseball League Unfolds

The LAB, which consists of six teams representing five different sports clubs, is a winter baseball league and the first semi-professional league in Argentina. Two associations, Federación Cordobesa de Béisbol representing my home province, and Liga Salteña de Béisbol, representing the Salta Province, formed the league to allow Argentina to be represented on the international baseball stage. Although we have six teams at the moment, my goal is to expand the competition to Buenos Aires to evolve into a nine-team national league, which could happen in 2021 or 2022. Even though the league is currently considered semiprofessional, the objective is to reach full professionalization in ten years' time. The goal is to nurture Argentina-born players.

We played our first season in 2017, and in 2019, we debuted in South America's Latin American Series, a professional baseball tournament featuring the champions of Colombia, Nicaragua, Panama, Curaçao and Mexico.

Argentina opens the Latin American Series with a Sound WIN!

On January 26, 2019, I cheered on Team Argentina, represented by the 2018 Argentina League Champions Falcons from Córdoba City, in its debut in a professional tournament. Team Argentina gave the first big surprise in the Latin American Series defeating the Tobis de Acayucan of Mexico. The duel was resolved in 10 innings before an audience of more than 10,000 people and the presence of the local Governor Cuaitláhuac García.

Our Argentinian crowd watched, on the edge of their seats, until the game was decided in the tenth inning when, in an 0-0 tied game, Gonzalo Cabanillas hit a single to center field, then stole second, took third on a passed ball and scored on a sacrifice fly by Leandro Juárez, giving the victory to the Argentines in their professional international debut.

Ultimately, the Leones de León of Nicaragua became the champions, with Mexico's Tobis de Acayucan the runners-up. Still, we felt proud of our showing in the Latin American Series. The organizers cancelled the 2020 Latin American Series in Panama City, Panama because of the coronavirus pandemic.

After a successful debut in the Latin American Series, my goal is to take Argentina and the league to the international level for the next cycle of the World Baseball Classic. I believe in goals and the importance of goal setting. Organizations and teams need goals.

The Argentine Baseball League promises to revolutionize the activity through the professionalization of the sport, the dissemination and development of a competition of a higher sports level and more attractive to fans.

Some former big leagues like Luis Sojo, Marvin Bernard, Wilson Álvarez and Alex Cabrera, coaches like Marco Mendoza and Pete Caliendo and current renowned players like New York Yankees catcher Gary Sánchez and Tampa Bay player José Alberto "Cafecito" Martínez have viewed the project with good eyes and support the idea for Argentina to one day make this dream come true. I want Argentine baseball to break out of its amateur phase and blaze its own trail in the professional world, all the way to the World Classic in the future. I want to see the first Argentine player in the Major Leagues.

Argentina has a long history with baseball, and it is a lifelong passion for me.

The one thing I learned and live by is that no matter what hurdle you face, there are four important things to help you fight:

- Passion
- Hard work
- Discipline
- Resilience

I think baseball helped me to become more resilient because no matter what you do you are going to fail...you will miss a ball ...you will get struck out...your coach will put you one day in the bench...and you need to keep going, waiting for the next opportunity.

Like life, you will be alone, you and the ball and nobody else.

Team Argentina celebrates as they upset Team Mexico

Pablo gives back to Argentina baseball with his hard work and passion for the game he loves.

I met our next contributor, Omar, when Pablo called me seeking recruiting assistance for his new league in Argentina. What a pleasure meeting Omar and what an outstanding ballplayer. He ended up winning the MVP for the championship series, but I was most proud of his professionalism. He truly helped move professional baseball in Argentina in the right direction

Chapter 13

Trust in God and Play Like You Did in Argentina by Omar Prieto (Puerto Rico/Argentina)

Omar, MVP with a smile and another Championship

By Omar Prieto. (Puerto Rico/ Argentina)

Born and raised in Puerto Rico, I am the youngest of three brothers. Ever since we turned three years old, we all have been practicing sports. We all started with baseball and later we tried basketball. I wondered which sport was the coolest. I tried basketball first but running back and forth was too much and you could tell that I was not going to be tall at all. After trying basketball and realizing I did not like running, I chose baseball. Sure enough, I made the right decision.

In our household it was always music and sports. My dad has been a professional musician since he was seventeen years old. Growing up, we went with our dad to his rehearsals and saw how important it is to be in sync with the band and for us it would be with our teammates. It taught us a lot, because we started to translate those same vibes to our teams. Thankfully, every team we played for appreciated us. The lesson was the better you work with your team together, the better the team will perform.

Our family was a team as well and our mom never missed a day working in the concession stand. She was always willing to spend countless hours in order to raise money for the teams we played for. My brother and I always felt gratitude, pride and respect towards our parents because we saw how they sacrificed their time and spent their money so they could drive us all over the island and buy us all the equipment needed to practice our sports. The respect and gratitude we felt drove us to give the best we could at all times. Fortunately, my brother and I worked hard, focused on baseball, and stood out in the little leagues, giving my parents a reason to smile and feel proud of us.

I was fortunate enough to start my international career in 2010-11 at the age of sixteen, when I transferred schools from Puerto Rico to Florida, going to an international boarding school called Montverde

Academy (MVA) where almost 75% of the students were not born in the United States. Here is where I started to actually learn English because I did not know the language at all. It was such a challenge that my roommate in my first year was from South Africa and my roommates in my second year were two Brazilians. In my first year I got to play with the current star for the Cleveland Indians, Francisco Lindor. I personally learned a lot from him about his work ethic and the way he played the game. The next year in 2012, I graduated out of MVA aiming to continue my education in a college in the United States.

However, I failed to find a college in the U.S. and started my bachelor's degree in Puerto Rico. After a year back home in PR, I found the opportunity to transfer to a school in Atlanta, Georgia for spring 2014. I was lucky enough to start right away and find some success. At the end of the year, I ended up winning MVP of the team. As soon as the spring semester was over, I transferred to a community college in New Jersey called Cumberland County College. 2014-15 was a year of a lot of struggles and challenges, including injuries, unstable grades, and fighting for playing time. The program, which helped me develop mental toughness, was great. However, I could only play within the program as a freshman and/or sophomore and I was already a sophomore.

Later in the summer of 2015 after taking a few weeks off from baseball and anything school related, I decided to transfer to Concordia University in Ann Arbor, Michigan (NAIA) where I was meant to finish my bachelor's degree and my college baseball career. During my years in Concordia everything clicked. I was able to get good grades and perform well. As a junior I was able to win the second team all-conference in spring 2017 and get invited to play in a summer league located in Quebec, Canada.

Summer 2017 was a blast. I was able to visit several places and compete against great talent. I took all that positive momentum and kept working hard to finish strong in spring 2018. That spring definitely did not disappoint, and I could say that it was a special senior season. I got to hit a walk-off home run on my father's birthday and a week later I hit another walk-off home run. As a team we had a great run and I ended up getting the first team all-conference, runner up for conference player of the year and second team All-American.

Days after my season was done, I travelled to Saskatchewan, Canada where I played my final collegiate summer league. We started undefeated 14-0 breaking the league's record on wins in a row. It was probably the most complete team I have ever been a part of. We had a great run, and I went out to play like I was playing in my backyard. Everything was fun and I accepted all the challenges with a smile on my face.

While finishing the season I received the offer to play in the Liga
Argentina de Beisbol (LAB). The timing could not be any better! I
signed with Pampas de Salta where I became the first Puerto Rican
born to play in the league. My teammates made the transition from
Canada to Argentina a smooth one for me. It took me some time to
adjust to the lifestyle because Salta is 1,152 meters above sea level.
However, after making that adjustment, I was able to perform at my
best, winning the Champion Bat and MVP of the regular season,
and later in the playoffs I got picked up by Falcons de Cordoba
where we won the championship.

Omar chats up "Blue"

Scott Weaver helped me start my international professional career. He gave Pablo Tesouro a hand to fly me from the US to Argentina. Also, he always kept in contact through my time in Argentina, giving me support and motivation to keep improving and having a good attitude towards my experience in Argentina.

After accomplishing the first season in the LAB, I got chosen to be a part of Team Argentina that was going to represent in La Serie Latino Americana 2019 in Veracruz, Mexico. We started the tournament playing against the top team of Mexico beating them in the 10th inning. I did poorly in my at-bats, so poorly the winning pitcher of the night, Yoimer Camacho, came closer to me and told me, "Hey bro, play like you were playing in Argentina, nice and relaxed. Just have some fun and trust God because he controls everything for you."

I listened, and I changed my mood. Yoimer Camacho helped me develop emotional intelligence. I was glad to get advice from him, and he did not lie. I finished the tournament on a high note, hitting a grand slam (first home run in a professional tournament by an Argentinian team), hitting over 400 average and being the RBI leader of the tournament. This was my best experience lived in a baseball atmosphere.

All those great accomplishments took me to Metz, France where I spent the 2019 summertime playing with the Cometz organization. Metz is a great city close to Germany, Spain, Luxembourg, Belgium and Switzerland--not too bad for my first time in Europe.

My experience playing the Cometz was awesome and very special to me. We played the First Division French league for the first time and we were always very competitive. Even though we could not make the playoffs, we showed that we were always a team to beat because we never gave up. We had a ton of fun in the car rides and our native French teammates took time out of their days to show us around the city and some of the countries around the border. It was a blast. I could say that I learned a lot about the game, and I had the chance to spread some of my baseball knowledge to the kids, which to me is very important and necessary for the good of baseball.

Later in 2019 during mid-season I got the chance to play in the LAB once again and this time was way easier because I already knew the place and the people. Scott Weaver encouraged me to play another season in Argentina. He gave me another chance to extend my international baseball career for another season. Scott definitely gave me another chance to live the dream. I am forever grateful to him. He is a great human being that cares and supports other people without asking anything in return. Because of his encouragement, once again, I became "Campeon de la Liga Argentina de Beisbol," making this the second in a row and finishing 2019 in a winning way.

Omar. Winning and family.

2020 started a little differently. I chose to play a semi-professional league in my home country Puerto Rico. I signed with Potros de

Santa Isabel where the people live and die for their team. Even in practices there were fans checking the team out. The few games we got to play, there were a lot of emotional games where I picked up on the fans' emotions and personally loved the way the fans felt about the games.

I have been blessed to play this game that has given me everything. I learned English, I have travel and I spent the best experiences of my life because of baseball. Trusting in God was the right decision, and I am also grateful to my family for encouraging my love of baseball. I am forever grateful.

Asia/Australia: Journeys from Tokyo, (NRT) Japan.

Chapter 14

Koshien Japanese Baseball by Scott Weaver

As stated, one of my goals while flying around the globe was to take advantage of my short layovers—sometimes I would have only 24 hours to sniff out local baseball! Our trips from JFK to Tokyo were a prize trip and often went to those who had seniority. Subsequently, I had only a few opportunities to fly trips to Japan. We originally were flying to Narita, an airport located in the northern suburbs of Tokyo. Later American Airlines was given a landing slot to Haneda, an airport located on the south side of Tokyo, in the small industrial village of Yokohama.

On one of my rare trips to Tokyo, I got to the hotel, took a two-hour "combat" nap, and when the jet lag kicked in at around two o'clock local time I woke up. After years of flying internationally, one of the lessons I learned was to sleep when you're tired and get up and out when you're not. When awake, I had to force myself to do things. Every time I flew into Haneda, I would go out and explore Yokohama, Tokyo.

Tokyo Giants Stadium. 2013.

Some guys take tennis rackets, mini-guitars, golf clubs and some even bring foldable bicycles. As far as I knew, I was the only one I've ever flown with who would take a baseball glove and a couple of baseballs. On an earlier trip, I had some success in the local park near our hotel and found a few guys throwing a ball around in the park. They were happy to have me join in. That was a step up from my efforts to find baseball action in Japan online. In the past, I had success in locating local teams in both London and Buenos Aires using online searches, but for some reason I had trouble in Japan.

On this particular trip to Yokohama, during a very hot July day, I walked through the downtown and into an electronics shop, something similar to a Best Buy, with flatscreen TVs, computers, cameras and cell phones. And in the background on the flat screens. I saw baseball being played. My first instinct was to determine if the game was live or taped, professional or amateur. Even in my jet-lagged state, I could tell the angle of the sun was about same. Must be live. Next, I noticed the players were young and most likely Japanese. But the stadium was a professional stadium with Japanese advertising throughout. The game was being broadcast live and in Japanese and when the box score was displayed, before they kicked me out of the store for staring at a flatscreen TV with no intent to buy, I asked the sales guy if this was a local team. And he said yes, they were playing at the Yokohama Stadium just five or six blocks away. He went on to say that this was the high school Koshien national tournament. I had found my baseball in Tokyo!

To my dismay, I noticed that the game was in the bottom of the ninth inning. Just as I sniffed out a game to go watch, it was about to end! And one of the premier sporting events in Japan at that—a unique experience for a layover.

Koshien baseball is one of their nation's biggest sporting events of the year. It's the equivalent of a Texas high school football championship played at AT & T Stadium, but bigger! All high school teams are invited to this play-all tournament, and the teams play multiple games until they have the national championship.

Most of the games are televised nationally. It's a huge deal! But I was disappointed that I missed my chance.

As I looked back at the flatscreen, I noticed one small detail as the cameraman scanned across the winning team's dugout. It was a detail so small that I'm not sure why it even registered with me. But as the game ended, I saw an equipment manager setting down a helmet bag. The helmet bag was full! And it could only mean there was another game. As a coach involved in numerous tournaments, I had done the exact same thing. Bring the gear down in front of the dugout and make a quick head nod to the coach to let him know he is in your space now.

Japanese Baseball Hall of Fame and Museum

The stadium was only a twelve-minute walk away as I now walked with purpose. I bought a ticket for about 2,100 Japanese yen or about $20 USD. Not cheap for a high school game, but what did I care. I was going to watch a nationally televised baseball playoff game in person!

When you first walk into a baseball stadium it has a certain feel to it as if you're walking into a French cathedral or museum. Having flown domestically for 18 years, I took every opportunity to visit as many stadiums as I could and consider myself a bit of a "stadium snob". To see the green grass and the openness of a place like Camden Yards, Wrigley Field or Fenway is breathtaking. Some think my hometown stadium for the Washington Nationals is fantastic, but I don't see it that way. No real view of the monuments and left field views of concrete parking lots. San Diego's, San Francisco's, Seattle's, Miami's and even Cleveland's stadiums top D.C.'s in my opinion.

Scott and Japan's Home Run leader Sadaharu Oh. 2013

Today, I walked into the Yokohama Baystars Stadium with a capacity of just over 34,000. Tight compared to MLB standards. All dirt infield. Not a good look. But as I was settling into my seat, I did notice the approximately 10,000+ fans in the stadium. Nowhere near sold out, but this was high school baseball!!

Tokyo Stadium. Bunkyo-Koraku. Japan. April 18, 2013.

After the disappointing look and feel of the dirt infield, I noticed and heard the high school bands play as if this was a football game. Each side would play their school's fight song or some type of cheer but not at the same time as the opposing team, as this would be disrespectful. My second observation was the beer and sake vendors. Yes, beer and sake sold at a high school game! What a great country! All the vendors were young girls in their late teens and early twenties, wearing short cover-all type uniforms, their hair pulled back with star glitter on their cheeks. All smiling and selling beer and sake at a high school baseball game!

"Tsumetai biru," I sheepishly asked. I can order a cold beer in a half dozen countries around the world. The young vendor handed me my beer and I sat down to enjoy the start of the game.

The passion and the love for the game was beyond anything I'd ever witnessed before. As a coach/manager, the first thing I noticed was the respect the players had for the manager. At the end of an inning, the defensive players would race to the front of the dugout and receive the instructions from the head manager. Then they would bow their head "hai" (yes) at the plan. I imagined it must be something like, "We're going to get base runners on, this is our strategy." He was like a sensei of a martial arts class, but it was being executed on a baseball field.

The base coaches themselves were not adult coaches, but they were student-athletes or player-coaches. Between innings they would meet behind the home plate and at a certain time they would sprint to the first and third base. Something you'd never see in the U.S.

The game ended with a 6-4 win from a small school in the northern region of Japan. It was well played and well executed. They didn't play just small ball, trying to advance runners with bunts or trick plays; instead, they played all aspects of the game and they played it well.

I stayed until the end of the game, which was now about seven a.m. body time. But what I observed at the end of the game stayed with me. The players, coaches and fans showed respect for the umpire. He was treated with the utmost respect, and his judgment was rarely challenged. When the game ended, all the players lined along the third base and first base line respectively. They acknowledged the umpire with a bow and the umpires bowed in return. The players turned and acknowledged each other's fans in appreciation as the leaders of each band took off their hats and accepted the thanks from the players. Finally, the teams turned to acknowledge their own parents and fans in appreciation. What an exceptional sign of gratitude by all involved, but it wasn't over yet.

As I headed up the steps to leave the stadium, I noticed the losing team had brought a small sack or bag about the size of a camera case. Each player bent over picking up dark black dirt from the infield as a remembrance of their time on the field. It was as if this was their temple and this might be their last opportunity to step on this hallowed ground again.

That was one of my last trips to Tokyo. I transferred to Miami which doesn't fly to Asia, but only to South America and Europe.

I met our next contributor, Lisa Maulden via David Burns and his "Baseball Jobs Overseas" and fell in love with her passion for the game she loves- softball. She's a ballplayer and has the mindset of a fighter pilot in every sense of the word. She'll fill in the gaps that I witnessed watching an only a few games in country as she starts her second year of professional softball in Japan!

Chapter 15

Salt and Sake: Pursuing Your Passion by Lisa Maulden (USA/Japan)

By Lisa Maulden. Softball Director of Operations, Baseball Jobs Overseas, Ogaki Minamo Softball Club, (USA/Japan)

Dear baseball and softball players: You are playing a sport of failure. When it comes to being successful within this sport, three out of ten times per se, that still means you have to fail the other seven times. Statistically, even with a 70% rate of "failure," you're still an absolute rock star.

Nowhere else in life are you able to have that type of percentage and still be considered successful. For example: in your relationships, in your everyday life, with your family, or with your boyfriend or girlfriend; if you only pick up the phone three out of ten times, you're not going to make anybody happy. If you're working at Starbucks and you only make three out of ten good coffees, you're definitely going to get the boot, especially if you're working in Seattle. I should know, because I was born and raised in the Pacific Northwest I discovered my love of softball around the age of 12 - thank you Coach Joe Jimenez - eventually played softball in college at Seattle University, which led to me professionally playing softball in Japan now. Along the way I have had to learn how to embrace and overcome failure.

Lisa, her coaches (Tom Milligan and Joel Pricco) and teammates (Emily Ferguson, Jordan Straughan, and Samantha Jimenez Jackson) who represented Maple Valley from Tahoma Little League through to Tahoma High School's varsity team

Being able to deal with failure is something a lot of athletes struggle with at first. We're very fortunate to play a sport where we can continuously learn from the game itself and from one another. You have to overcome failure and learn how to pull your head out when things are going as planned. That starts with adjusting your mindset. The majority of softball is a mental sport. Trust your training, trust the process, and most importantly, trust your gut. I tell import players just that in my role as the Softball Recruitment Manager for Baseball Jobs Overseas.

Lisa playing first base for Seattle University

No matter what you're doing in life, as long as you are happy and you are pursuing something that you are passionate about, I am totally 110% for it. Everybody's different. Everybody has their own things that they love and that they like. I preach pursuing your passion a lot while in conversation, especially with prospective imports. When I was in college my walk-up song was "The Pursuit of Happiness" by Kid Cudi, which helped center me and remind me to continue to chase what truly makes me happy. Choosing to be happy and pursuing happiness is just that: an active choice.

Nowadays I gravitate more towards the phrase "pursue your passion." In pursuing my passion for softball, which started out as a way to afford college, I feel like I've grown as an individual, both on and off of the field. I feel like my five years playing overseas in Australia, New Zealand, Europe and Japan has helped me grow and become the person and player that I am today. I made a choice to go overseas after graduation in 2015 and have benefited from it ever since.

I can confidently say that choosing to pursue an international professional sports career is less than "traditional" among most Americans. I've chosen a path less traveled by and one that is hardly understood or supported amongst my peers and family members.

As a result, I found myself in Japan, playing primarily a designated hitter role (selected as one of the "Top 9") in the 2020 season for the Ogaki Minamo Softball Club in Ogaki near Nagoya in the 2nd Division Japanese Softball League. Even after a shortened season, greatly impacted by the coronavirus pandemic, we placed 1st in league competition and were rewarded through promotion to the top league for the upcoming 2021 and 2022 seasons.

2021 Minamo Captain Mariko Sudou creating a pile out
of salt in the entryway of our dugout

Salt, Sake and Softball

During our last practice before the holiday break here in Japan, I noticed our team captains started putting little salt piles at the entryways to the dugouts. Simply put, I've seen a lot of interesting or "strange" things while being overseas.

As curious as I typically am, I was watching them and thinking to myself: "Whaaaat exactly is going on here? Have they gone nuts? I think this time they might have actually lost it…"

My captains noticed my curiosity and informed me that this was a traditional way to say thank you for the successes of the past year and to welcome in the New Year with success for the upcoming season.

We continued to put salt piles in the dugout and other significant places on the field: at our positions, in the bullpens, etc. The girls then gave me a little handful of salt, advised me to go to my position, first base, and make my little pile of salt. The girls then went around and poured sake on each of the salt piles to complete their thanks to the field. This was probably one of the most memorable things I got to experience and be a part of during my time here so far. You can just see the emotion that the girls have behind these types of acts, and that's something I will not forget. These types of moments are the ones that I will remember for the rest of my life.

Lisa posing with her salt pile at first base at the
team's home ground in Ogaki, Gifu, Japan.

I am thankful that the girls typically include me in these types of celebrations and don't instead say, "You know, this is kind of a Japanese thing." They normally are very warm and welcoming and remind me that I am just as much a part of this team as they are, even though I am a foreigner. There is a team respect and a sense of team spirit called *wa* here in Japan. Upholding and respecting the team *wa* is of utmost importance, both on the field and also within the Japanese culture as a whole.

In America we are thankful and respectful towards our peers and our sport, but it's entirely different here in Japan. From my experience, this comes from the culture and their history. Wherever we practice or play a game, we always remember to say our "pleases" and "thank yous," but Japanese style.

For example, in Japanese softball and baseball, we show acknowledgment and gratitude for the field, umpires and other league officials, coaches, players and the fans throughout the game. When we arrive at the field, we set up for warmup, have a meeting about the day's plan, then lineup from tallest to shortest in front of the dugouts. The captain is always at the front of the line and will say, "*Onegaishimasu,*" and then bow to the field in a respectful manner of "please have a good day here at the field," and the rest of the team will follow. On game days, after warm-ups and before the game officially starts, we typically line up from home plate to the pitcher's plate instead of in front of the dugout. Due to the coronavirus pandemic, we have to abide by social distancing rules, and this is one of them.

The umpire will call, "Game!" This signals our captain to say, "*Onegaishimasu,*" bow to the field/the other team, and then the umpire, while we follow her lead. After the game or practice is finished, we line up again and say, "*Arigatou gozaimashita*" as we bow, "thank you very much." If there are fans in attendance, whether it's a league game, practice or a scrimmage game, we bow and acknowledge their presence and support as well.

Ogaki Minamo Softball team thanking their fans for their support
after the final game of the 2020 season in Kitakyushu, Japan.

I can't emphasize enough the importance of respect in this country. Respect for the club, staff, teammates, fans, all the way down to the equipment and the ground that we use every day for training. As Americans, when we are shagging balls, we kick them into little piles to speed up the cleaning process – and because, realistically, bending over that many times is just not in the cards. In Japan, using your feet to corral or kick the balls - or any equipment - is a huge no no and is considered disrespectful. It's very refreshing to see the appreciation for absolutely everything, down to what we Americans would consider as the little things.

It's also amazing to see the country's support for this game at the youth level, the high school level, the collegiate level, and also at the professional level; it's truly a whole new world. I've only been to one baseball game so far and I'm pretty sure it was not even the top league. But the things that they're doing at these games - the cheerleaders in the outfield while people are warming up between innings, mascot races, light shows, and fireworks post-game - are the most fun I've had at a baseball game in years. They actually live and breathe baseball here. The players, the coaches, the fans, everybody. It's an amazing environment, to say the least., It's especially refreshing coming from America where baseball is our national pastime. But for the Japanese, baseball is not their national sport historically. They've made it into something that is pure entertainment for the entire country, while also being played at a very high level.

This experience has been one hell of a ride so far. The best part about it all? We've only skimmed the surface.

The Learning Curve

Being a sponge is one of the top characteristics anyone possesses. Being able to consistently learn and know that learning is never done is a beneficial and an admirable quality. Here in Japan, they play a completely different style of softball. This is because it is in accordance with their body type and their culture. If you look at the framework between female athletes playing collegiate softball in America and female athletes playing collegiate softball here in Japan, you're going to notice a lot of differences straight off the bat through appearances alone. Specifically, in terms of muscle mass, height, and body shape/type per athlete, etc. The Japanese have completely changed the way that they swing and the way that they throw to suit their strengths as individuals and as a generally more "petite" class of athletes - at least in comparison to us Americans. Learning and experiencing these differences and similarities firsthand between the styles and cultures can only benefit myself in the long run, both as an athlete and as a future coach.

Lisa having a laugh with her teammate and practice partner Miyuki Fujii before a league game.

Lisa and her teammate Mizuki Imagawa sharing a moment
while on a team road trip to camp in the Japanese mountains.

What I quickly noticed from my first week here in Japan was these girls were all work and little to no play - they are completely dedicated to their sport and to their work with little to no time for themselves.

First of all, here's a day in the life. On a normal weekday, the girls go to work at their respective sponsor company in the morning from 8 am to about 11:30 am or noon – myself included, but twice a week instead of all week. After this, they report to the field shortly after 1 pm. I typically rock up on my bike around 1:15 pm, help set up for practice (lay out gear needed for warm up and practice, pick up trash around the field - in fall, leaves on the ground are considered trash… - etc.), stretch, and wait for our *shūgō* (pre-practice meeting) around 1:45 pm, then our bow. After our warm-up jog (usually 10-20 minutes), and our team dynamic warm-up and running (25 minutes-ish), we go into "catch ball" and "toss," which starts our defensive practice.

Depending on the day and what part of the season we are in, we will spend time doing various types of *nokku* (fungo) for 2+ hours before spending our break time setting up for hitting. We are to warm up on the tee in pairs, move to front toss, then typically set up for rotational hitting off of live pitching and machines. We typically hit for 2+ hours as well, depending on light and what the plan is for the day. Normally we have conditioning or running training on the days where we do not have lifting, and also team dinner, which gets us home around 7 pm or 8 pm.

Lisa showing her respect for the opposing team during opening ceremony of the 2020 season in Ogaki, Gifu, Japan. PS check out the smiles of her teammates - she must have been doing something right!

On weekends, we typically have our *shūgō* around 9 am, lunch around 1 pm, and finish sometime between 3-5 pm. Typically after any practices or games, you can find the girls still taking additional reps, whether that's fielding, hitting, etc. Their dedication to the process and to the sport is unmatched.

Another takeaway: At times, practices can be more quantitative than qualitative. In American terms, we like to get in and get out – aka, quality over quantity. In Japan, the latter is the preferred design. For example: over summer, Coach assigned us to complete 15,000 swings in 23 days.

Aaaallright.

My American brain's first response was: "You're kidding me, right?" But the *kantoku* (director) or Head Coach was not, in fact, kidding, by any means. Experience has taught me that the completion of this task will fall under a quantitative type of practice, and I wondered how my teammates would attack this task while also making it quality work. For them, completing 1,000 swings in a practice is difficult, but not unimaginable. Some struggled more than others to stay focused and have quality swings throughout, which is to be imagined and understood.

Lisa counting her coins to check how many swings
she had completed up to that point in the day

For myself, I couldn't keep track of tally marks in the dirt, let alone 1,000 per day. I created a coin system where 1¥ (yen) was 10 swings and 5¥ was 50 swings. My family knows I am not a fan of coins, but this was a perfect use for these pesky wallet weights. This also served as an incentive. After doing a set of swings, I would put coins in a bag, and move on to the next set of 20, 30, or 50 swings. This way I was able to go off of my feelings instead of chasing a number. Once I started to feel my swing going to shit, I stopped, counted my coins, and that was it for the day.

I have a different style, and yet I am an absolute fan of my teammates. I catch myself just watching them do their thing sometimes, as they are amazing individuals and athletes. During the games I can sometimes see that their quantitative practice preparation gets them into a bit of a pickle and their nerves can sometimes get the best of them. The thing to realize is that nervousness is okay and can be tamed or suppressed through the right types of mental training.

As I said before, you have to be able to overcome failure in this sport and overcome it quickly. Sometimes if I feel like I've really fucked up, I'll take a moment to grab some dirt, take a moment to look at the outfield, and once that dirt is released, the moment is gone as well. I try to help the girls trust in themselves by being vulnerable and acknowledge that I do make mistakes as well. Everyone has their own way to release and deal with pressure. These releases are formed through trial and error in pressure situations.

So far with my Japanese team I have found myself in a mentorship role - which I really enjoy. With this being said, they sometimes don't realize that I am learning just as much (or more) from them as they are learning from me.

Chalk Talk

Teammate Rina Abe holding the tape measure to ensure accurate base length for a camp in Gifu, Japan.

Playing here in Japan, we've played and practiced at some very interesting locations. A lot of the times we play on baseball fields and there is a fence brought in or made at our distance. Most of the time during the weekend if we don't have our regular field, we will go to what I can best describe as a sandlot, or a dirt soccer field. The girls are experts at marking off and creating a softball diamond for the day's use, no matter the conditions. This typically involves a few tape measures, base pegs, and heaps of chalk.

It's amazing to watch, as they know the exact measurements and even mark off a fence on the days where it's needed. Surely, if you ask anyone else to complete this task, they would more than likely eyeball the base length and say, "That's good enough for me!" One day we were playing a scrimmage on a baseball field with no fence. These girls measured and marked off the fence line with cones and put balls on the cones. If the ball went through the fence during the game, then the outfielder could grab the nearest ball off of the cone and resume play like nothing strange had just happened. Honestly, these girls have thought of it all and never cease to amaze me.

The Japanese respect the team and their culture through continuous awareness of the team's *wa*. They do not refer to our manager and our head coach by their names at all. I call them by their first names because that's how they introduced themselves to me, and that is easiest for the foreigners. The girls will typically call the staff by their position, rather than their names. For example, my head coach's first name is Mochizuki. The foreigners and I call him Mochi, while the rest of the team refers to him as *kantoku* (director). The same goes for our GM. As a whole, there is a very respectful culture both on and off of the field. There is a hierarchy within the team comprised of the *senpai* (upperclassmen) and the *kōhai* (underclassmen). The girls also speak and treat each other respectfully, especially when talking with their elders. Every day, as players and coaches arrive at the field, they are greeted with *konnichiwa* and a small bow. No matter what we are doing, when staff, club members, or people of importance arrive at the field, we all stop what we're doing to greet them to acknowledge their presence. With this being said, after a successful season, one by one, the coaching staff and the captain are lifted up in celebration by the members of the team.

Head Coach Takao Mochizuki being lifted up by the 2020 Ogaki Minamo Softball team members after winning league and being promoted into the top league of the Japan Softball League for the 2021 season.

Another thing that I find interesting is that our head coach will coach one base, and a player will coach the other base. We don't have a staff member coach the other base. Rather, it's typically one of our bench players. This happens during all of our games, both league and scrimmages. During practices, we like to scrimmage and also do game simulations. The hitter will give signs from the batter's box to the runners, so everyone is on the same page. This was very hard to adjust to, as giving signs is hard enough as it is, but giving signs while also trying to focus on the game scenario as a hitter is fairly tough adjustment.

Food for thought regarding quality vs. quantity: in my perspective, if you make practices the hardest part of the sport, the games will become easier and more fun. If you are able to target those game-like, pressure situations and simulate them during practices, this can only help your team. By making practices the hardest part of the sport, you're preparing your athletes for the potential adversity that they may face in the game.   If you have athletes that struggle mentally during games, targeting and building their mental toughness during practices is something I would highly recommend giving a go. During the game, you should be having fun, enjoy competing alongside your teammates, and trust your training.

Mementos from Japan and Beyond

I tend to grab new opportunities by the balls, and I'm someone who embraces change. I absolutely love change. Some people, when I talk to them, will say, "Oh, I can't bring my dog overseas? I can't come." It's three months, maybe six months. What are you holding on to at home that you can't leave behind for three to six months?

For me personally, I would much rather live my life to the fullest and completely embrace the moment. The way I see things, I can only play competitively for so long. I don't know how it's going to end, if it's going to be on my terms or on God's terms. I want to make sure I'm living in the now and I'm living in the moment, and I want to continue to share my passion for the game with the youth and my teammates while I have the opportunity to do so. Almost anything that you're doing at home right now, you can be doing in a foreign country. I think people fear the possibility of failure and also the fear of missing out on things that happen back home while they're gone. If you are not making life changes that don't scare you a little every so often, are you even living?

In the USA we are very familiar with the "rat race" that is our society. We get up, make our coffee, go to work at the 9-5 job that we don't exactly enjoy, go home, have dinner, just to do it all again the next day. There's also this imaginary timeline that you have to graduate from high school, go to college, find and marry the love of your life, graduate, have kids, etc. Professional athletes, especially those who are international, do not follow this timeline, which scares "normal" people. Typically, people-pleasers look to tick the above boxes at all cost, to show that they are on the "right path to success." Well, individuality also shows through how people go through life.

After my first season overseas, I returned home to teach and to coach, which is what I really thought I wanted to do with my life post-softball. Days, weeks, and months went by and I could feel that I was making an impact within the local community, but I wanted to do something bigger. This drove my decision to return overseas in June 2016 as a player/coach and I haven't looked back since.

Being a professional athlete and running around the world is not something that everyone would be fond of. Typically, I would receive comments, mostly through jealousy it would seem, as I'm "avoiding the problems back home," or statements similar to this. At the end of the day, I am following my passion and my heart and I am making an impact overseas, which is what is important to me. Things have upgraded over the years, as I now have a salary-paying job, full time insurance, an apartment, and a club full of amazing individuals. This is much different from European ball or ball Down Under, where your salary is just pocket money for food and/or beer, and not much more. The latter scares people and keeps individuals within the rat race and chasing the hours and the paycheck at the job that they hate, instead of pursuing their dreams.

Lisa in a Kimono

One of my regrets is that I wish I would have started traveling earlier in my career. When I first went overseas, I focused on the sport only. I was reluctant to make deep connections with my teammates, as I knew the moment was only temporary, and I didn't spend my off time wisely. Nowadays, I've learned to take advantage of the time off and to spend as much time with my teammates as they can stand – both on and off the field.

Fortunately, the girls on the team here in Japan include me, a *gai-jin*, which is a big deal.

Typically, on my off days I enjoy doing day trips to places to see more of the local country and culture, while taking longer vacations when the opportunity presents itself. This past Christmas vacation here in Japan I ended up going to Kyoto, Osaka, Miyajima, Hiroshima, Lake Hakone, Tokyo, and Ueda, which is the Nagano area. It was a very rushed trip at times, but I also got to experience more of Japan (outside of softball related trips) in those two weeks than I had in the nine months I'd been in the country so far.

Senior Day Flowers

Every country that I've played in I have met lifelong friends. The people in the clubs, the imports, the families I've stayed with, I still keep in touch with those people and they are near and dear to my heart. I truly invest in the places and the team where I play. When you go and live with people overseas, it can be very hit or miss, but if you are a people person and if you try to understand what is going on in the local culture and local families, you'll make friends for life. Every time I leave a contract somewhere, I leave a little piece of my heart as well, and it sounds so cheesy but it sounds so true. I am certain I will have lifelong friends or *tomodachi* here in Japan as well.

Teaching and Learning Curve, Revisited

I definitely love when prospective baseball and softball people reach out and ask me about my experiences overseas. One of my favorite things to give advice on is during the negotiation process between the prospective import and the club. This involves looking over contracts so both the imports and the clubs can understand what they're signing up for. Some people think what they're walking into is completely professional and some people think that it's just backyard bullshit. It definitely depends on the country, the club and the league. Everybody is different in what they want and expect from an experience overseas. Being able to communicate with the imports and the clubs and try to find the right match is sometimes difficult, but, in the end, when things are all signed, sealed and delivered, it's super rewarding for all parties involved: the import gets an opportunity to continue their career, to travel, to be exposed to a completely new way to play the game, while the club gets a new set of eyes and a key player for the upcoming season. That, to me, is what you call a win-win scenario.

Additionally, you are the sum of your experiences, which is what makes everyone so unique and beautiful in their own ways. No matter how many times you bring imports to a club, no two imports will impact the club in the same way. Each plays the game differently, and they all have different coaching philosophies because they each come from completely different baseball/softball backgrounds. Using the import's knowledge and passion for the game at a grassroots level – within the schools or within the youth of the club – is an irreplaceable experience, for both the youth and also for the import, and is of high importance.

Japanese Team Selfie

I always listen to other players and their reasons for playing. My "why" for specializing in softball from a young age was because I wanted to earn a college scholarship to help me pay for school.

Now, I continue to play this game for many reasons, including my love for this sport and the adventures that come with it. If you look at other countries around the world, the reason the majority of these athletes' play is for their love of their country, or simply as a hobby, for the love of the game. I always enjoy talking to my teammates who choose to play this sport, as softball is not generally a major sport, even in the USA. This also allows me to get to know my teammates on a more personal level, which typically builds team camaraderie. I discover more about people, which in turn leads to exploring myself as a person.

Lisa Junior Fan

Whether you are in a classroom or on a ball field, learning is not a singular path. Everyone on your team is individual. As a coach, I know it doesn't make sense to expect everyone to complete their 15,000 swings in the same way. It was the same in my teaching career. There's not one way to learn that is more effective than others. This is because some people learn better through doing, while others through seeing, etc. I can say, "Keep your hands inside the ball," "hit the inside seam," "rock the baby," and any of these phrases are explaining the same thing motion-wise but they are being said in a different way that makes sense to different individuals. As an educator, I try to remind the students to reflect on sessions and write down things that made them say "ah ha!" or things that made the light bulb go off in their head.

Everyone has an individual role within a team. Your individual strengths are going to be backwards from the guy sitting next to you. My strengths are going to enhance other people's weaknesses and my weaknesses are going to be enhanced by other people's strengths on the team. That is what defines a team. A team is essentially a sum of all of its parts; a large puzzle, if you will. Knowing your role within a team is very important as well, as every team has a specific make up and direction in order to accomplish their goals.

At the end of the day, always choose to push through your failures, as the process so looks much sweeter on the other side. Lastly, however you choose to show gratitude and give thanks, always remember to do so along your pursuit of happiness.

THANKS

I'm thankful for an opportunity to continue to play, especially through the pandemic. Thinking about athletes in particular, they have a timeline. They are only able to play competitively or at a high level for so long. My heart breaks for those athletes who've been forced into retirement because their seasons have been lost due to the pandemic, or those who have to wait an entire year to compete in the now 2020 Olympics.

David Burns and Lisa

I'd like to especially thank David Burns for posting my blog back in 2015, which started my overseas career, and also for bringing me on board with the Baseball Jobs Overseas crew in 2017. A thank you to each of the club's that has hosted me over the years and has brought me into their softball families. PS that shirt is forever lost in Salzburg after the umpteenth "car bomb" we had in town.

Thank you to: Kurtis Tomkins and Tomoko Goda, for both encouraging me and advising me in your own ways on this amazing Japanese journey; my dad, for understanding and supporting this crazy dream of mine from the start; my mom, for throwing me whiffle balls in the front yard and doing **whatever** it took to set me up for success; and my sister, my biggest fan and supporter, thank you for dealing with my bullshit over the years and for holding down the fort while I've been away. I miss you all so dearly and hope to see each and every one of you in the near future.

Lisa's family and support

Chapter 16

The Mental and Physical Aspects of Pitching by Scott Weaver and Eric "Lefty" Niesen

By Lt. Col. Scott "Hurler" Weaver and Coach Eric "Lefty" Niesen (USA)

Let's break it down. There are two aspects of pitching that directly relate to flying a supersonic jet like the F-16: mechanics you adhere to and the mental approach to the job. Flying a jet is not a simple matter of going through the proper steps, nor is it a matter of using your own instincts – a sort of "fly by the seat of your pants" approach. Instead, it's a very mechanical and measured plan to land "bombs on a target," or "bullets on your enemy." In the same way, the mechanics of proper pitching are critical for both the success and the health of the pitcher. Poor mechanics increase the risk of serious injury. A pitcher uses mechanics to locate a fast ball, curve or slider to a specific target.

Both live in three-dimensional worlds. Pitching mechanics are illustrated in the two diagrams on the left; flight mechanics on the right.

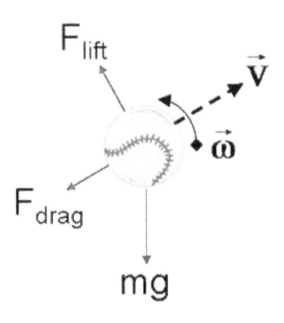

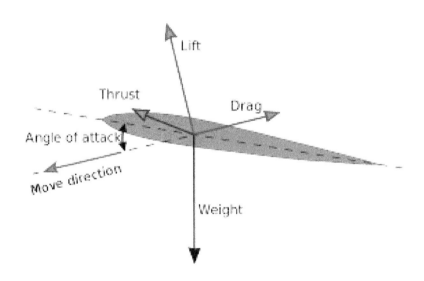

"Lift and Drag" ref. aerodynamics of a
baseball and wing. wikipedia. 2020.

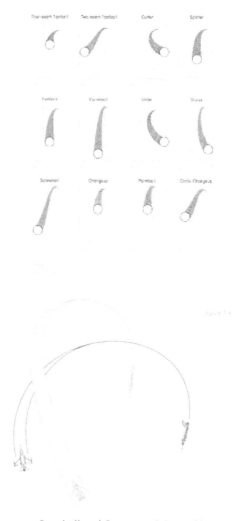

Baseball and flying in a 3-D world.

Mechanics Explained. Think about it. A fighter pilot's combat arena is a three-dimensional world composed of up, down and trajectories involving various levels of speed. There's a relationship between

167

speed, direction and accuracy. The result can be devastating if a fighter pilot misses an objective.

Parallels with Baseball. This same type of approach can be seen in the game of baseball – especially now with the increased use of in-flight tracking technology. This new technology, such as Trackman and Rapsodo, closely tracks the precise flight of a baseball. Interestingly enough, the Trackman technology was created using missile defense strategy. As a result, the two worlds of fighter pilot training and baseball coaching become eerily similar. Just as a pilot needs to know how to fly his aircraft to evade or attack an object, the pitcher needs to know how his pitch moves in space in order to pinpoint his intended target.

Baseball uses spin rates, spin axis and up and down movement patterns to perfect a pitch. In truth, the same forces that apply to airplanes and lift are the same forces a pitcher will use in make a pitch move in a purposeful way.

As we've illustrated, pitchers also work in a three-dimensional world. Though they are just 60' 6" from their target or opposing hitter, and the speeds at which they throw are much slower than supersonic, pitchers still work in the world of up, down and trajectories at various levels of speed. In the case of a pitcher, a curve ball that just hangs in space, without the speed, is just a two-dimensional attempt that probably gets crushed by the hitter!

Chapter 17

Destined to Play the Game by Matt Blackmore, (Australia/Czech Republic)

International All-Star. Matt Blackmore.

By Matt Blackmore. Melbourne Demons Baseball Club(Australia/Czech Republic),

My baseball journey started when I was running around the bases after watching my dad play locally where I lived in Melbourne, Australia. Dad was a five-time MVP of his club and joined his father as the only father-son duo in the club's best players throughout its eight-year existence. The baseball club was the center of his world. My father actually met my mother at an after-game party held by my mum's parents at their house. She lived behind the right field home run fence at the Moorabbin baseball club where my granddad was the president and her brother Tony played. My Uncle Tony represented Australia during his playing career also.

You could say I was destined to play this amazing game we all live and breathe. Then one day as an adult, I received a fateful phone call. My friend Ashley Young explained to me a coach was looking for a pitcher, position player for the season ahead in the French Elite competition.

In the space of two months, I was on my first European bound flight to Paris to meet up with my teammates from the Bois Guillaume Woodchucks based in the Normandy region of France. Living with a French teammate and his girlfriend who both didn't speak English was something I was going to have to overcome quickly.

Because the teams in French baseball in the elite division are spread out across the country, we took train trips and minivan trips through some beautiful landscapes and cities full of history and culture that date back hundreds of years.

The competition was of a decent standard with ex-affiliated baseballers filtered throughout the league as the import players. Each club was allowed two import players on the field at any one time unless the player had a European passport. Since everyone commonly used English with the imports, it was easy to strike up conversations and swap baseball stories, coaching kids and the unfamiliar living conditions, since most, like me, were away from home for the first time.

Returning to Europe the following season was always on my mind after getting a taste for it and the culture especially. I returned as a player / coach, which was new to me considering I was around 24 years of age and had never coached. I ran into some challenges. For example, the team and club had a different feel from the previous season, and even though I had excelled on the field, the team ran out of money and I was contemplating flying home because they couldn't pay me.

I met Gene Grimaldi, a baseball scout, at the Challenge de France in Toulouse and he mentioned something about a Prague Baseball Week in the Czech Republic. I stayed at his Paris apartment and the next morning we were both flying to Prague.

Prague Baseball Week was one of the coolest baseball experiences I've had. There was a round robin set up with teams from the Czech Republic, Sweden and Russia, and a softball competition on at the same time at the Prague Eagles Baseball Centre, an amazing setup with two baseball and two softball fields maintained to beautiful standards.

Staying with other imports from Europe who were there to make up their own team in the round robin, I met James Sanders, who was playing for the Zurich Barracudas of the Swiss League. One thing led to another and I found myself on a flight to Zurich with a severe case of food poisoning thanks to a pizza in Prague, missing my welcoming party to play for the Cuddas. Unfortunately, in my sick state, I slept funny on my throwing shoulder, never recovered from that night and wouldn't reach a high standard on the field for the Barracudas. I returned to Australia.

After another successful Australia season with no injuries, I received an email from Arnost Nesnal, the head coach of Draci Brno in the Czech Extraliga. A powerhouse club in the European baseball landscape winning 22 titles in a row at one point (CEB Cup, Czech champions, 3rd European Cup). Let's call them the Yankees of Europe.

To say I was excited was an understatement. I'd met some of these guys the previous year at the Prague Baseball Week tournament and these guys knew how to handle themselves. Might I mention that a double AA standard ballpark was built in the off season with a restaurant above and living quarters below allowing foreign players to live, eat, train at the field whenever they wanted?

I had many new opportunities. For example, the Czech Republic would be the first place I'd played to a TV audience with some games televised, especially against the local rivals Technicka Brno. Draci Brno also gave me the opportunity to play in the European Cup, a tournament where the best teams in Europe come together for a week in June and play off for the right to be crowned the kings of Europe.

We travelled to San Marino, a small country inside Italy where the sun was hot and the baseball was going to be even hotter. The team stayed in the seaside resort town of Rimini and practiced there before the cup's opening games.

Draci opening games included:

- Kinheim from the Netherlands.
- Solingen Alligators from Germany.
- Montepaschi Grosseto from Italy.
- Marlins Puerto Cruz from Spain.

Highlights for the team were playing competitively against all four big clubs and smashing Solingen 10 - 0.

A personal highlight was finishing in the top three hitters in the tournament with a .625, going 5 from 8. As well, throwing six innings against Italian giants Montepaschi giving up five hits and one ER, I finally felt like I belonged on a mound in Europe and could get some respect from opposing players.

Kinheim would defeat the Huskies of Rouen (France) in a close final viewed by a couple of thousand fans at the San Marino Stadium.

I was a two-way player for Draci. However, my hitting would slump throughout the year, although my pitching got stronger and smarter and helped the team win another consecutive championship by defeating another crosstown rival in Brno Express. I compiled a .50 ERA for 35 innings of work pitching in all of our final's appearances, finishing the year with around six saves and feeling a sense of pride knowing I contributed to this title, my second title in a senior men's league.

Returning home to Australia, I decided I didn't want to go back to Europe and opted for Australian rules football, soccer, again with my local team. I continued my summer baseball and the following season that European itch returned and took my game back to France and spent my summer with a different Barracudas team in the seaside city of Montpellier in the south of France. The Barracudas of Montpellier were a great ball club with a good mix of youth and senior guys with some of them still playing for their country. This time, I was in perfect health and the season was def extra special and my most enjoyable, made easy by the weather and great teammates. We partied hard during the week, came to play on game day and flew to the majority of games in Paris making us all feel like big leaguers. We made the finals but were bundled out to a red-hot Rouen Huskies who at this stage were creating a legacy in the league with several titles in a row.

I'd kept my fitness up during the Europe summer and my arm was feeling as good as it had ever felt heading into another summer season in Australia where I was once representing my state in the Australian league.

We won the national championship that year as well as representing my country against Chinese Taipei in a three-game series where I picked up a save. A moment I'll never forget.

The state of Victoria produced one of the best seasons a state had had in recent history. I'd won a national title in 2007 as a rookie. This was a sweeter victory as I had a big role to play as a senior member compiling a 7-1 record for 50 innings of work out of the bullpen. I was awarded the honor of pitcher of the year as well as MVP of the finals, throwing six scoreless innings of relief work giving up one hit and punching out seven. Another moment I'll never forget, witnessed by family and friends.

Believing my Europe baseball was finished, I received an email from Draci for one more crack at helping them win another title. The season was halfway through and I had to jump on a plane and get to Prague and meet the team to qualify. I stayed for two weeks and flew home where I'd wait a month and fly back to the Czech for the second half of the season.

The team played well, and I did my part starting several games and closing others on the way to my second Czech national title. The beers flowed and the party was large. I knew this was definitely the last time I'd suit up in a European competition.

I've met lifelong friends and visited many countries on the back of playing the game I love. I never would have thought in my wildest dreams that baseball would take me all over Europe as a paid profession.

I still play in the Division 1 men's competition here in Victoria at the ripe old age of 38 for the Melbourne Demons Baseball Club and still love the game I grew up with.

I do think about my time overseas most days and I'm thankful to all the teams that took a chance on me. There were some lows, but the highs outweighed that, and I wouldn't change anything.

Czech Republic Champions. Matt Blackmore.

Baseball uses spin rates, spin axis and up and down movement patterns to perfect a pitch. In truth, the same forces that apply to airplanes and lift are the same forces a pitcher will use in make a pitch move in a purposeful way.

As we've illustrated, pitchers also work in a three-dimensional world. Though they are just 60' 6" from their target or opposing hitter, and the speeds at which they throw are much slower than supersonic, pitchers still work in the world of up, down and trajectories at various levels of speed. In the case of a pitcher, a curve ball that just hangs in space, without the speed, is just a two-dimensional attempt that probably gets crushed by the hitter!

Chapter 18

Baseball Is Family by Alex Pike (Australia/Canada)

Alex Pike leads the London Mets to another Championship. 2008

By Alex Pike, Former London Mets Manager
(Australia/Canada)

I love baseball because baseball is family! My experiences playing baseball overseas has proved to me that baseball is a WORLD sport, and that the love of baseball will bring people together! Plus, baseball players are just damn good people. WOW. That got sappy REAL quick.

I've traveled the world and played baseball in many different countries over my 40-year life span! And probably the first question

I ever get asked no matter where I am when I meet a fellow baseball player is, "There's baseball in Australia?" The second question is, "How did you get into baseball?"

My answer to the first question is "Yeah, mate! Baseball is HUGE in Australia!" The answer to the second question is a bit longer. So, I normally say, "Buy me a beer and I'll tell you! "

Why baseball for me? Well, that's easy: the 1987 and 1991 World Series! I watched those live on TV as a kid back in Australia and loved watching Kirby Puckett, the legend. Also, I was allowed to stay up late for the first time to watch a game with my dad. Baseball is family.

Pikey doubles to the gap and drives in 2 RBI

I started playing for The Kensington Baseball Club (KBC) in Adelaide, South Australia back in 1986 when I was six years old and, well, I played every year till I was 27 years old! I asked my parents why they made me play baseball and they shrugged their shoulders. Whatever the reason, I am thankful for the reason I learned lessons I carry with me today. KBC was all about hard work, commitment and teamwork as well as being around damn good people. People underestimate that, and yet it's like gold. KBC didn't just play baseball—they created more of a community where they welcomed everybody!

Flash forward to 2007 when I turned 27. When I made the decision to leave Australia and move to London, United Kingdom, well, I didn't actually give it that much thought, to be honest. But two months into living in London I was sitting at my desk at work and it hit me: This will be the first year in 21 years I won't be playing baseball. That feeling hurt! I automatically spun around in my chair and typed London Baseball into Google and my next family popped up!

The London Mets!

I developed mental toughness to adapt in a new situation. Straight away I sent an email and requested to play! Pretty much instantly I found myself in an email conversation with Josh Chetwynd who gave me the once-over with twenty questions and before I knew it, I was invited to their next training session, which was on a dirt gravel soccer pitch in North London, but hey, British baseball! That year we went on to win the British National Title, and well, I was hooked. I settled into my new family for the next nine years.

Josh announced the year after that he was going back to the States and he needed to find a manager/coach for the Mets and as usual without any thought, I stuck my hand up and before I knew it, I was responsible for the Mets. Big shout-out to Carlos Diaz for being my right-hand man for the first couple of years and Robbie Anthony as well. The Mets became my new family and I embedded much of the KBC culture into the Mets during my time there. The Mets are now one of the most successful clubs in British baseball and, well, I'm going to be arrogant enough to say that it's because of the incredible club culture of KBC. When I took over the Mets, I tried to create a Club where people wanted to be a part of and then before you knew it you were playing baseball as well.

I met some amazing people over the years and travelled to many countries playing baseball due to the Mets and must say I am lucky to have created many lifelong friendships and memories because of it. Massive shout-out to Jon Carter and The Belfast North Stars and the Athletics Baseball Club in Attnang-Puchheim Austria. FINKSTONBALL! Wow, what can I say about that?? The stories! The people! The baseball! It needs to be on the bucket list of every player. I went there about four or five times and played with the Belfast North Stars. Finkstonball showed me that baseball is a world sport, since teams from all across Europe compete every year.

Now living in Canada with my beautiful wife, I am thankful for baseball for the people I have met, the places I have seen and the friendships I have created! Baseball is family.

Cheers, Alex "Pikey" Pike Forever chasing KBC

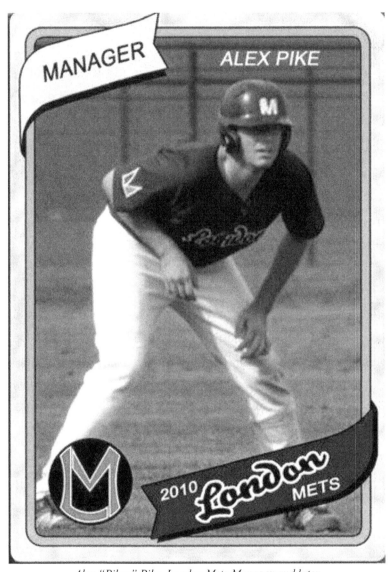

MANAGER

ALEX PIKE

2010 London METS

Alex "Pikey" Pike. London Mets Manager and later inducted into the Mets Decade Team. 2012.

Epilogue

It's an understatement to say 2020 was a tragic year for the world. Due to the pandemic, millions of lives have been lost, economic issues and joblessness continue, and even more mental health problems have arisen due to lockdowns and isolations. The game of baseball, which brings so many together and is an international language, is only one of the many things forever changed by the global crisis.

Our goal is to promote something constructive, to help spread the word to the millions of boys, girls, men, and women affected by this pandemic, and to further, in some small way, the growth of international baseball and softball. If reading this book and playing a rhythmic game of catch with your son or daughter, your teammate or wingman brings any semblance of health and normalcy to the world, then we have done our job.

In a broader sense, A Pilot's Passion: Baseball Travels the World is about finding and pursuing your passion in life. Make each day count. Seek out your adventures. Get out of your comfort zone. Go explore. Be a mentor. Surround yourself with people in your life with a passion, whether it's art, writing, cooking, fishing, golf, or even baseball. Find that emotional intelligence which helps live life in the present and focusing on the positives in our life for the future. Rise and Grind!

Hurler

Postgame: Where Are They Now?

Let me conclude this section of the book by thanking all my contributors. From Australia to Argentina, all of you showed your true passion for this great game of baseball and softball. No matter where home is or where you first picked up a baseball, your stories are amazing and should be motivation for others to follow in your footsteps.

Where are they now?

Matt Blackmore lives in Melbourne and still plays as a pitcher in the Victoria Summer Baseball League for the Melbourne Demons Baseball Club, previously playing for the Melbourne Aces.

David Burns lives in Austria. He is a player/coach of his local club team and is promoting baseball around the world with Baseball Jobs Overseas, facilitating an average over 300 connections between club and import every year.

Liam Carroll lives in the UK and is the former field manager for the Great Britain Lions, continues to coach and blog about baseball.

Chris Maloney is a baseball coach and the manager of the TITLE Boxing Club in Bethesda, Maryland, where he lives, and strives to help individuals with their personal health and fitness.

Lisa Maulden lives in Ogaki, Gifu, Japan and will play in the 2021 season for the Ogaki Minamo Softball Club. She continues to be the Softball Director of Operations for Baseball Jobs Overseas.

Eric Niesen, his wife and two children (4 and 2) are living in the Kansas City area where Eric is a private pitching coach.

Paul Perry continues to live in Buenos Aires, Argentina. He works as a writer, actor, and voice-over artist.

Alex "Pikey" Pike lives and works in Toronto, Canada with his wife. He loves life, cold beer and, of course baseball. He runs a Facebook group, For Love of Game, with 2,600 members.

Omar Prieto still lives in Santa Isabel in Puerto Rico and plays as a catcher for Potros de Santa Isabel and seeking playing opportunities around the world.

Pablo Tesouro lives in Buenos Aires, Argentina and still is the director of the League of Baseball Argentina and continues to grow the sport.

Jo Weaver lives in North Carolina with his girlfriend Claire. He is working full time, golfs and is still playing baseball.

Scott Weaver lives outside of Washington D.C. in Maryland with his wife and 14-year old daughter. When not flying, writing or researching, he is involved with supporting and mentoring aviators and ball players. His other interests include golf, hunting and he has recently purchased an experimental airplane called the RV-8.

For anyone reading who is interested in contacting any of these individuals or is in interested playing or coaching overseas please reach out to: Baseball Jobs Overseas.

Miscellaneous Photos

Second and third generation of pilots
Lt. Col.'s RC "Doc" Weaver and Scott "Hurler" Weaver. 1953 and 1984.

My daughter, Syb Weaver in Miami operations 2018

Buenos Aires. Sydney and London

"Fast" Freddy Badagnani, friend and baseball nut. Buenos Aires. 2016

Shankee team bus. 2017

Lisa and team mate: Kimono style!

Japanese welcome party

International sign for double okay!

Lisa and her Japanese friend

Champions seem to smile more.

Shankees flight back to Miami on the 777!

Shankees Win in the new uniforms!

Made in the USA
Las Vegas, NV
14 June 2021